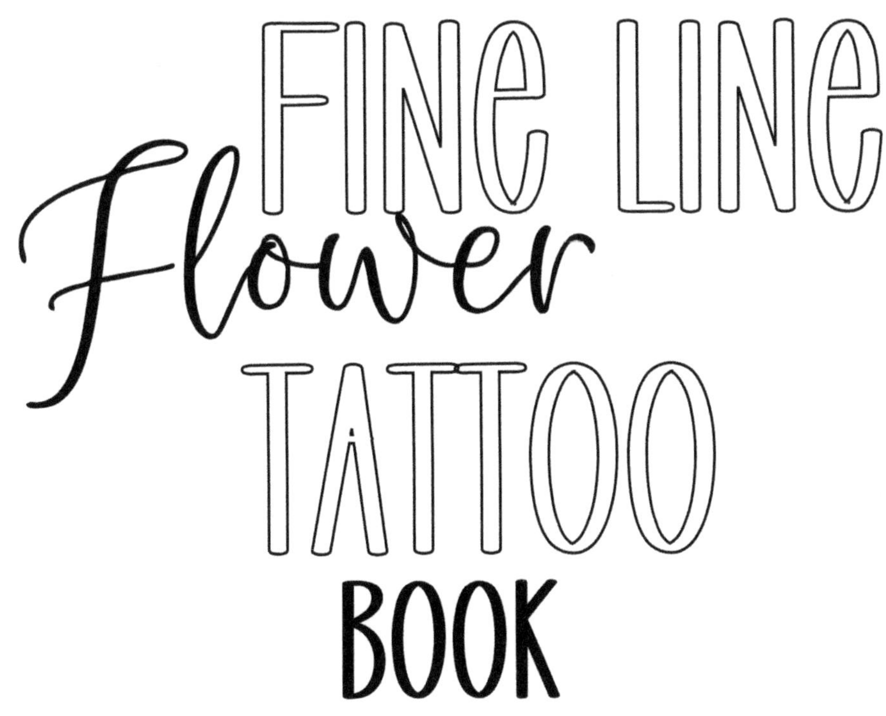

FINE LINE Flower TATTOO BOOK

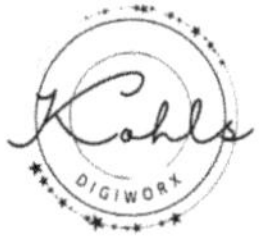

777 botanical tattoo designs

This tattoo template book offers a large selection of small, minimal and fine flower and plant tattoo motifs that are perfect for Fine Line, One Line, and the Single Needle technique.

One of the most important reasons for choosing a small tattoo is probably the beginner friendliness. These small designs are excellent, especially for people who have not yet had any tattooing experience and would like to familiarize themselves with the art of tattooing. Work and social environment often play a role in choosing a fine line tattoo, which can be worn discreetly in any walk of life or professional situation. They are certainly an eye-catcher.

After all, the mini tattoos offer decisive advantages:

Small tattoos and the duration:
The tattooing process does not take long and the costs are reasonable.

Small tattoos and the pain:
The pain factor also often plays a minor role with a small and fine motif, and should you ever become dissatisfied with your decision, the tattoos can easily be covered or removed by laser.

Small tattoos as a reminder:
Small tattoos are also so popular because they offer a good and subtle way to capture memories, for example of a vacation, a good friend, or a dramatic life event.

In recent years, several styles have been established that are explicitly intended for tattooing small designs or are at least well suited for this.

Fine Line:
It is probably the most common style when it comes to mini tattoos and it is usually the best for it. The Fine Line style is self-explanatory. The tattoo artist uses a needle that is as fine or small as possible for the entire subject. Shades and too many details are often avoided and the tattoos are mainly defined by minimalism and very delicate lines.

One Line:
The focus here is less on which needles are used and more on the fact that only one needle size is used. This type of tattoo can be done in a very fine way as well as with thicker lines. Since the tattoo consists of only one continuous line, there is no shading in this style either and the details are usually rather marginal.

Single Needle:
With a single needle, the tattoo artist uses the smallest possible needle size for the entire design. Accordingly, it is a combination of the first two styles mentioned. However, in contrast to the Fine Line, the Single Needle style is not exclusively used for small tattoos. It is also used for large designs. But unlike Fine Line and One Line, with this style, far more details and shades are possible and even important because the more contrast a single-needle tattoo has, the better it ultimately comes into its own.

Whatever technique you choose, this book provides 777 tattoo ideas that will help you find a trendy, small and floral motif to make your dream tattoo come true.

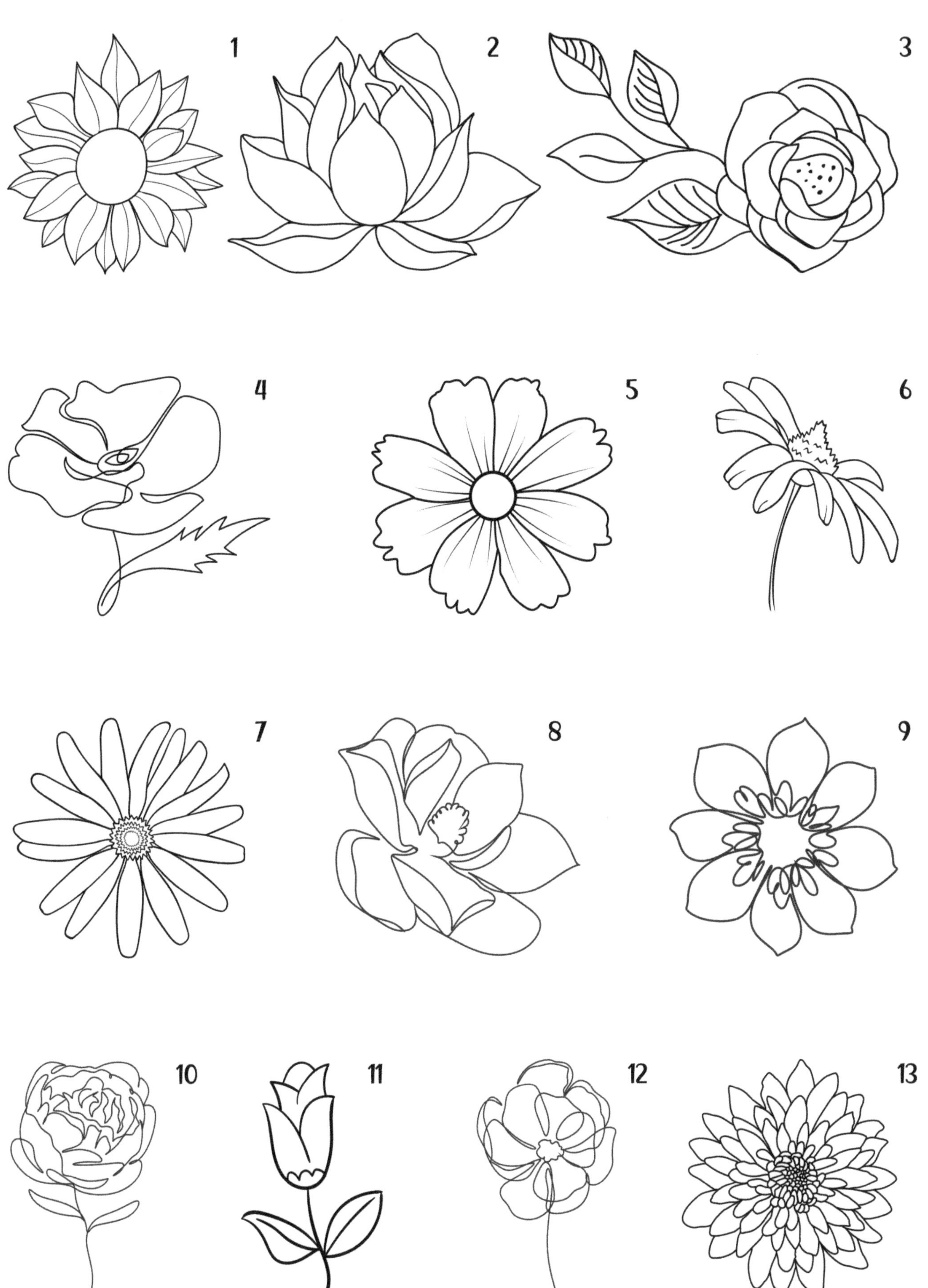

1
2
3
4
5
6
7
8
9
10
11
12
13

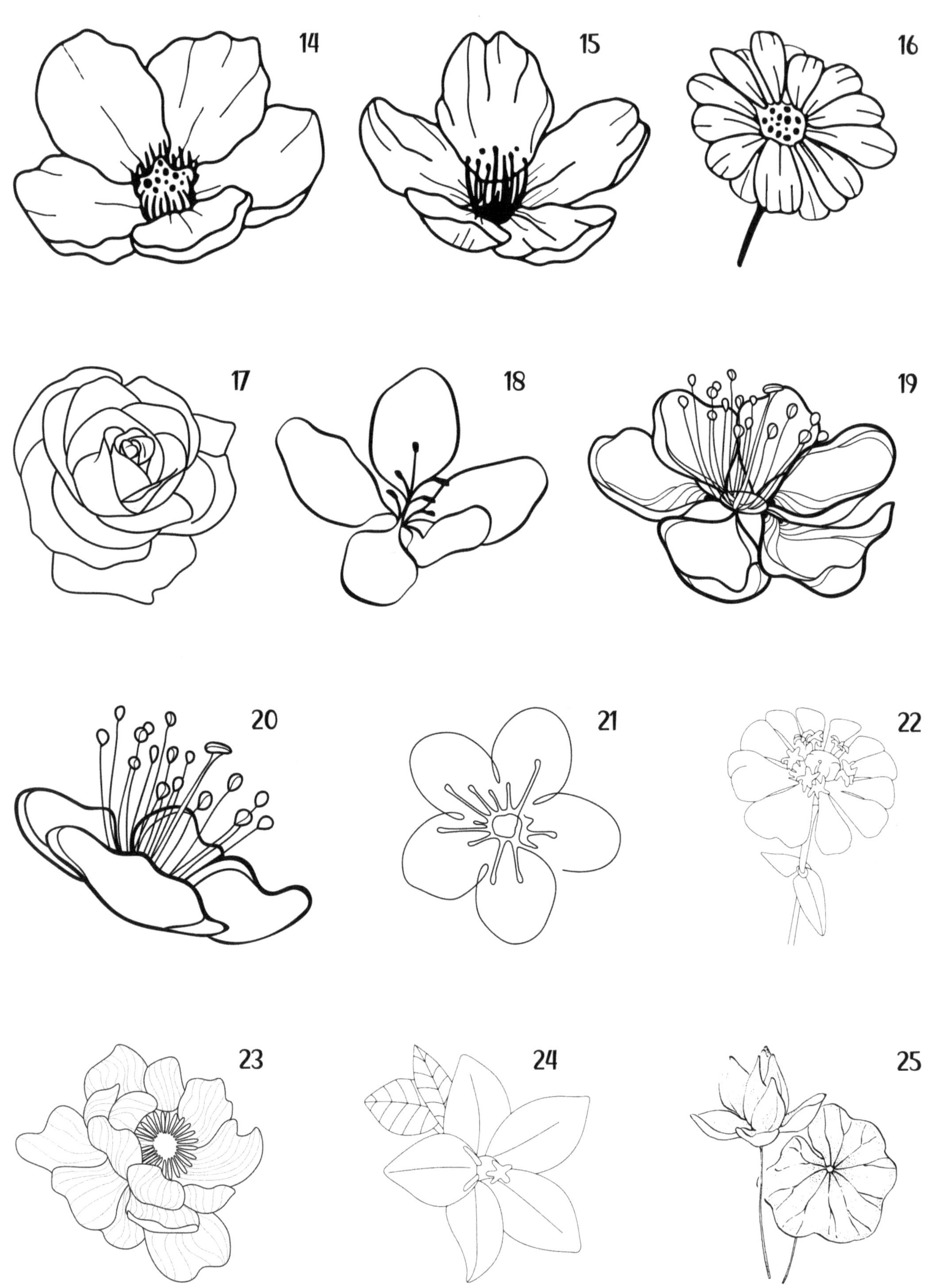

14
15
16
17
18
19
20
21
22
23
24
25

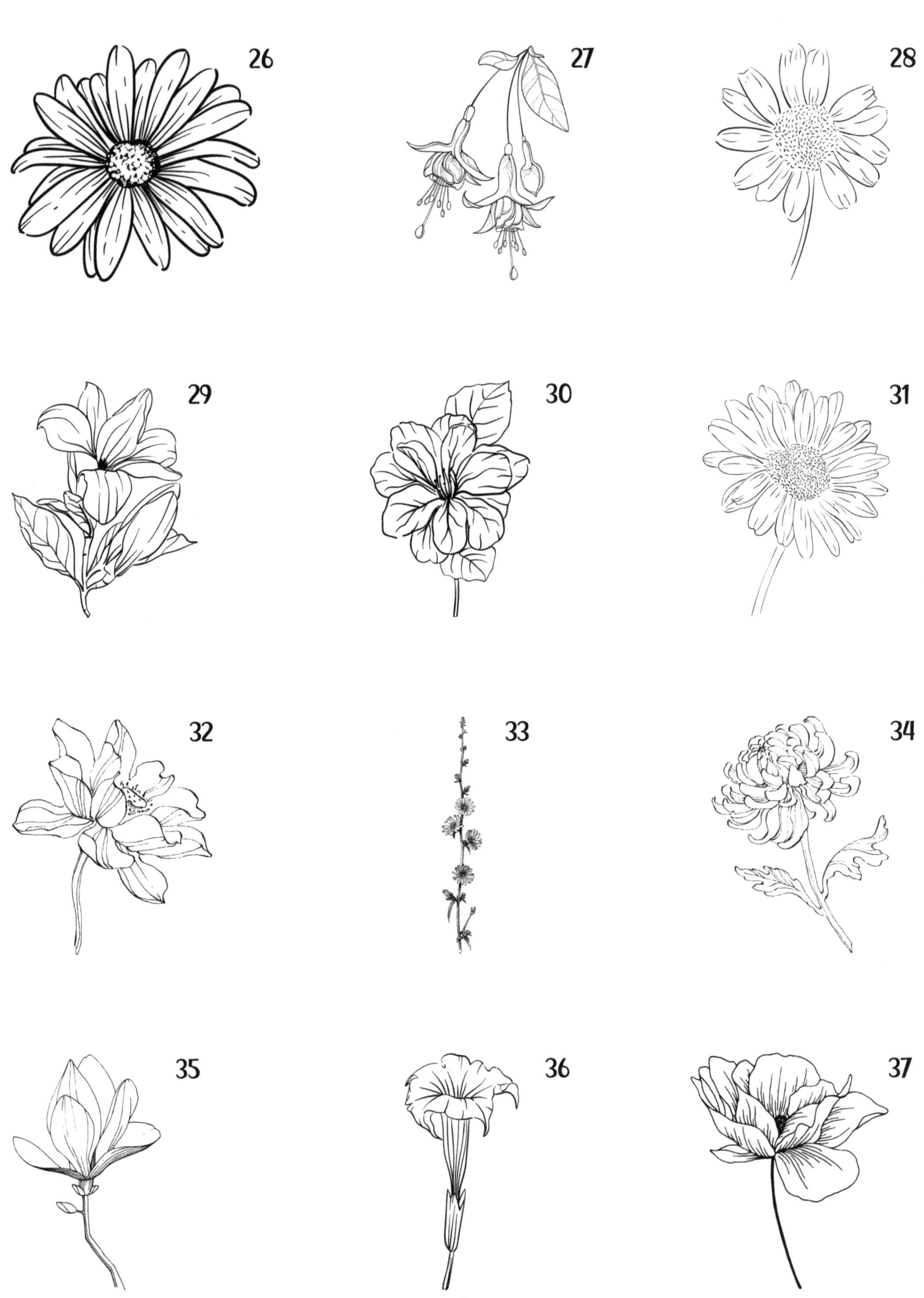

26
27
28
29
30
31
32
33
34
35
36
37

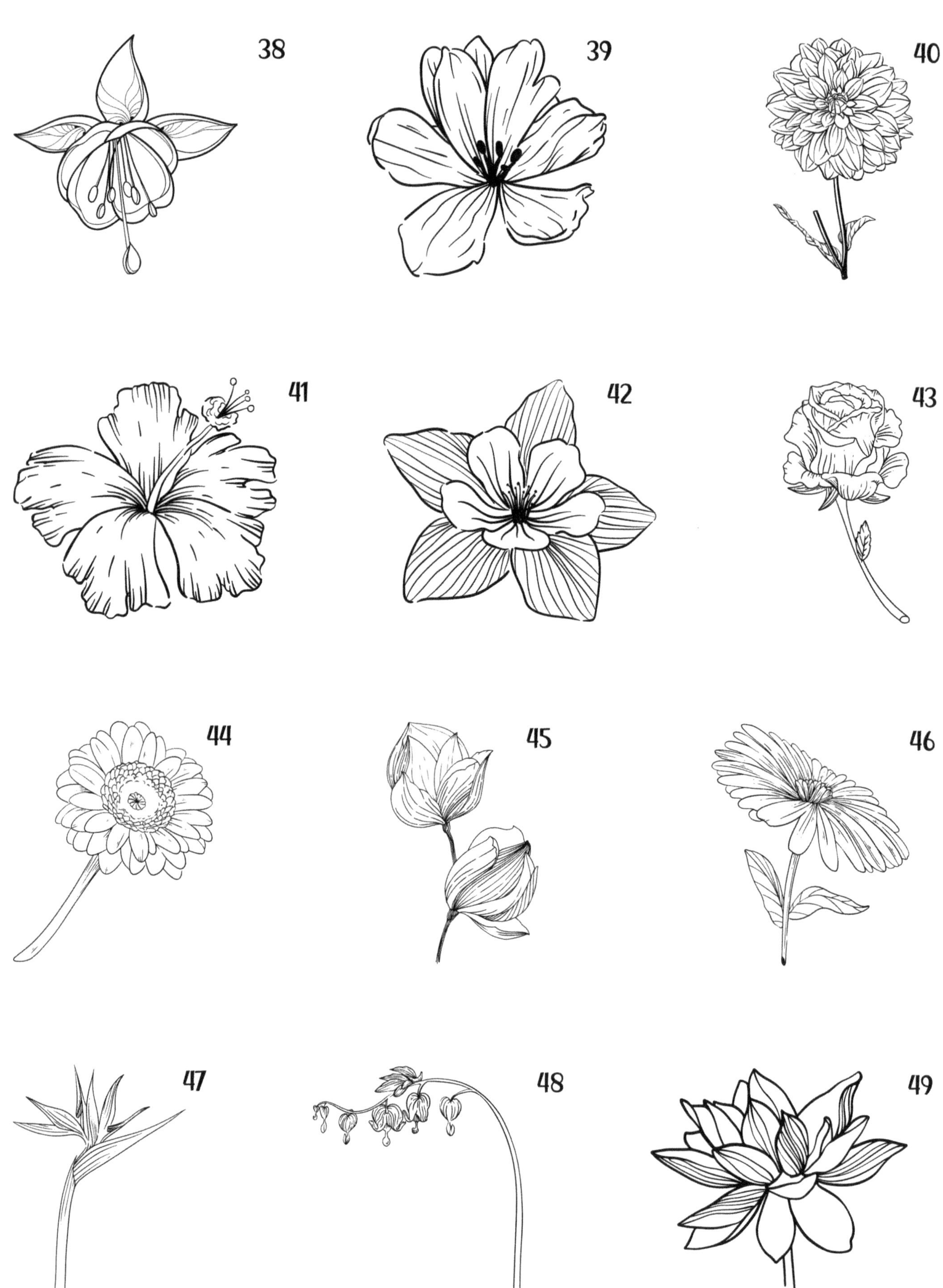

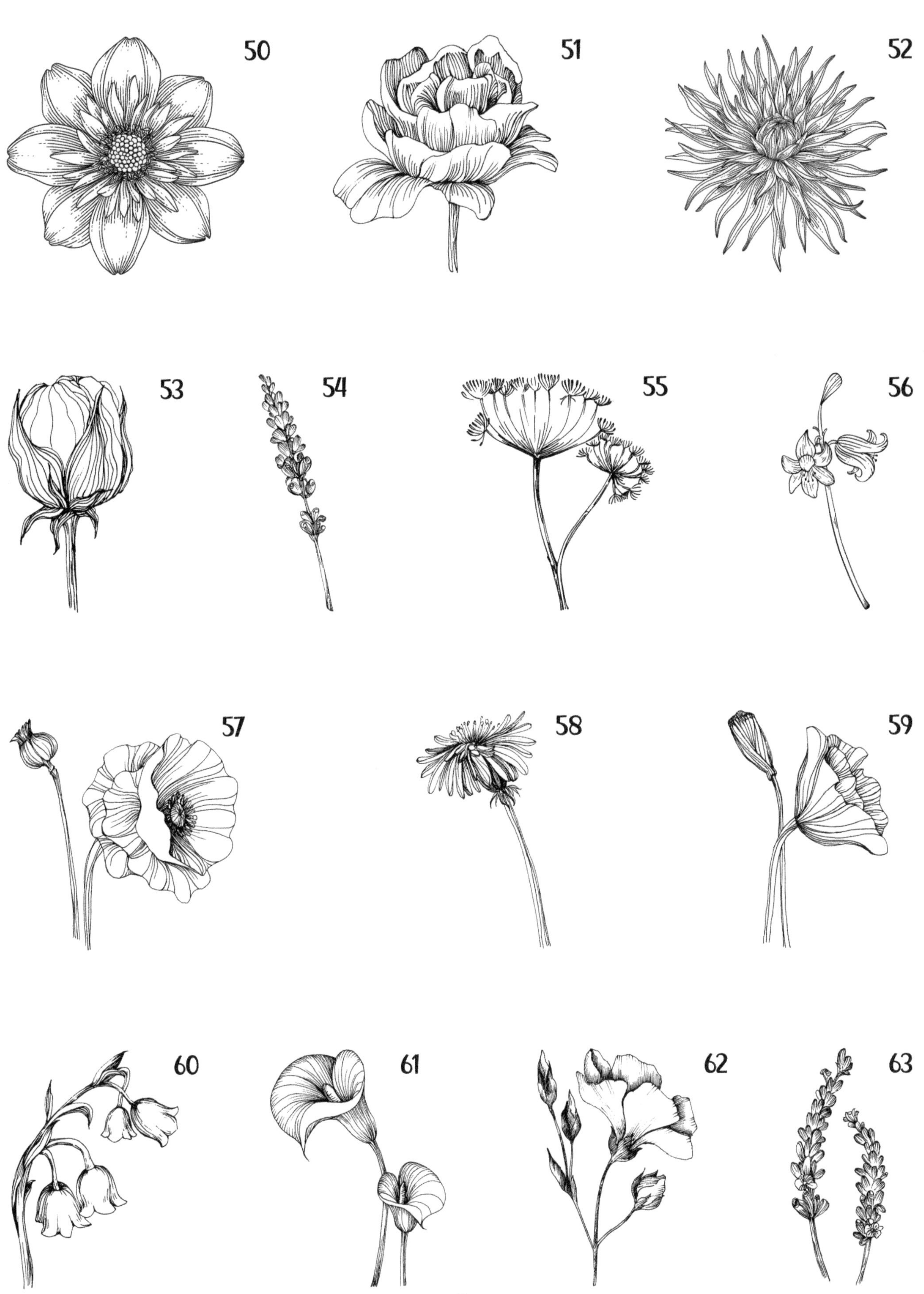

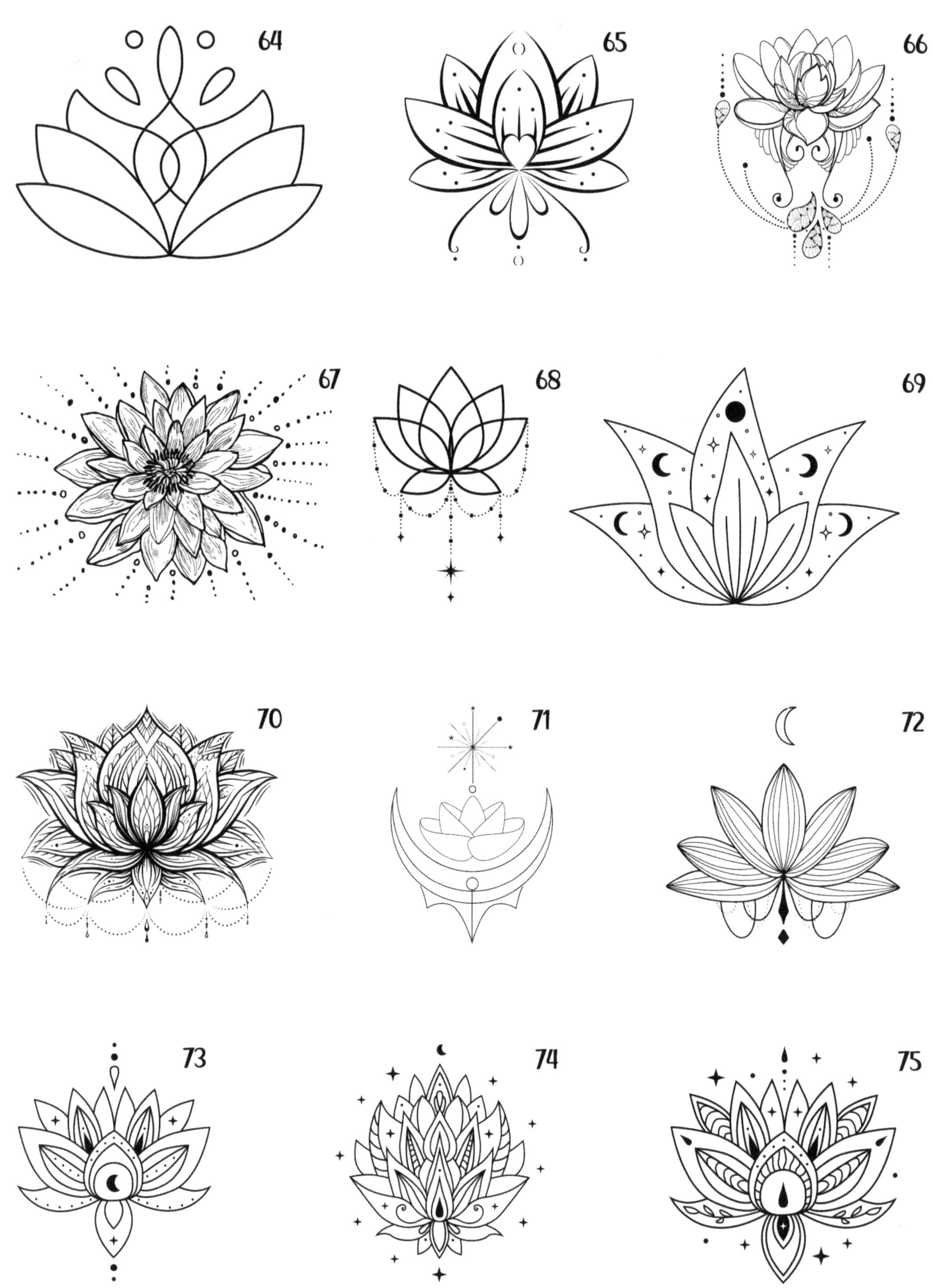

64
65
66
67
68
69
70
71
72
73
74
75

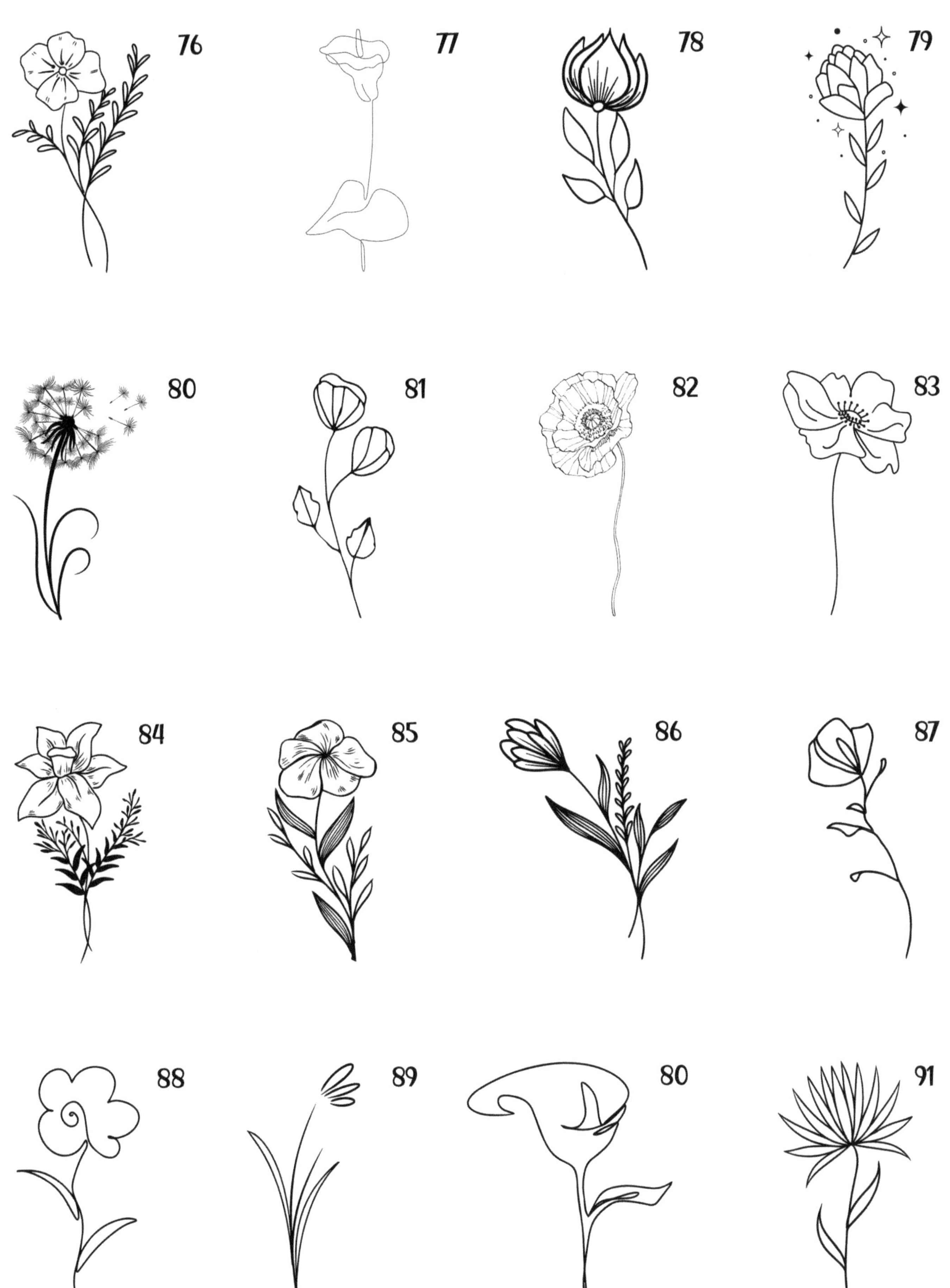

76
77
78
79
80
81
82
83
84
85
86
87
88
89
80
91

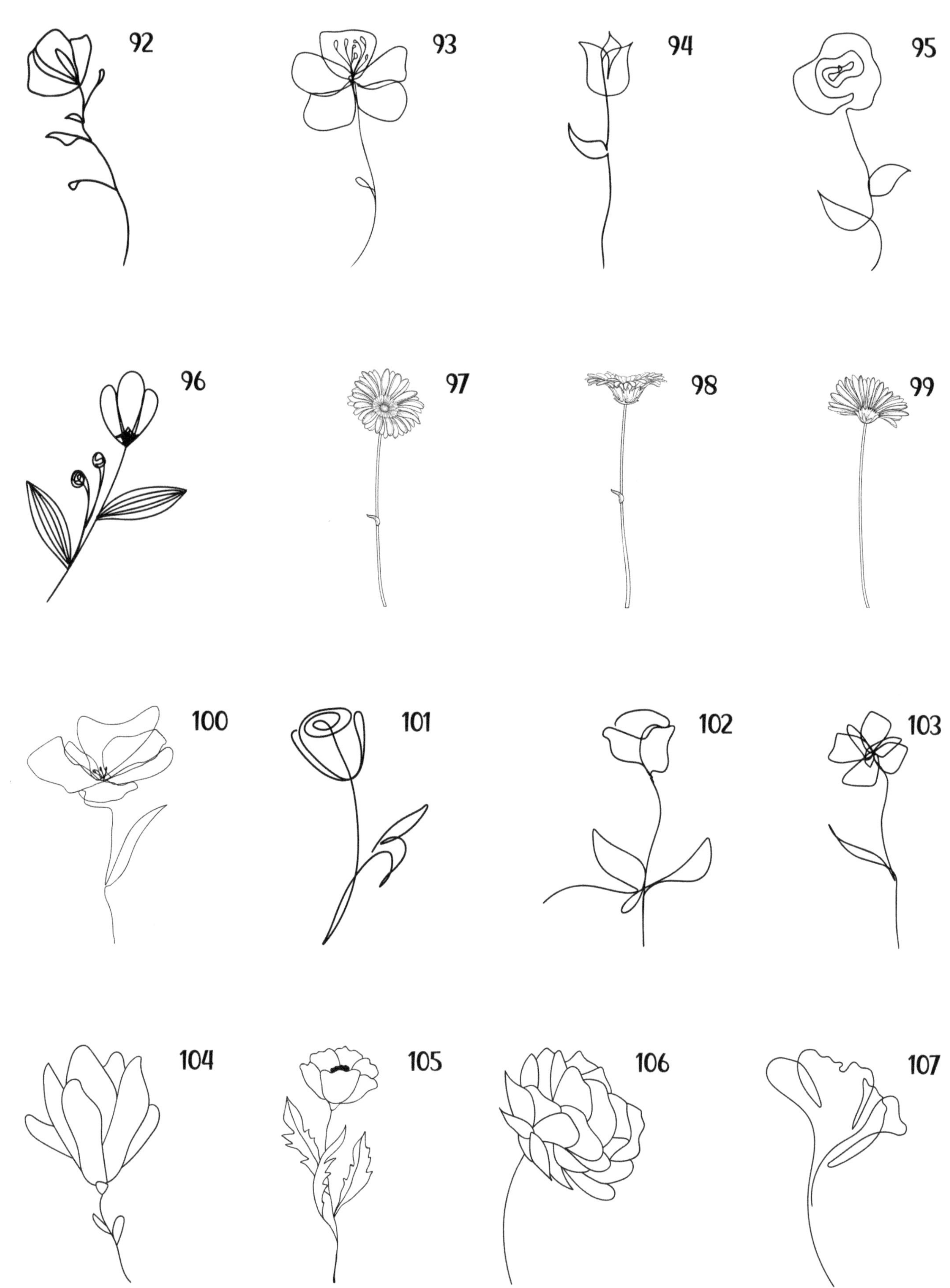

92
93
94
95
96
97
98
99
100
101
102
103
104
105
106
107

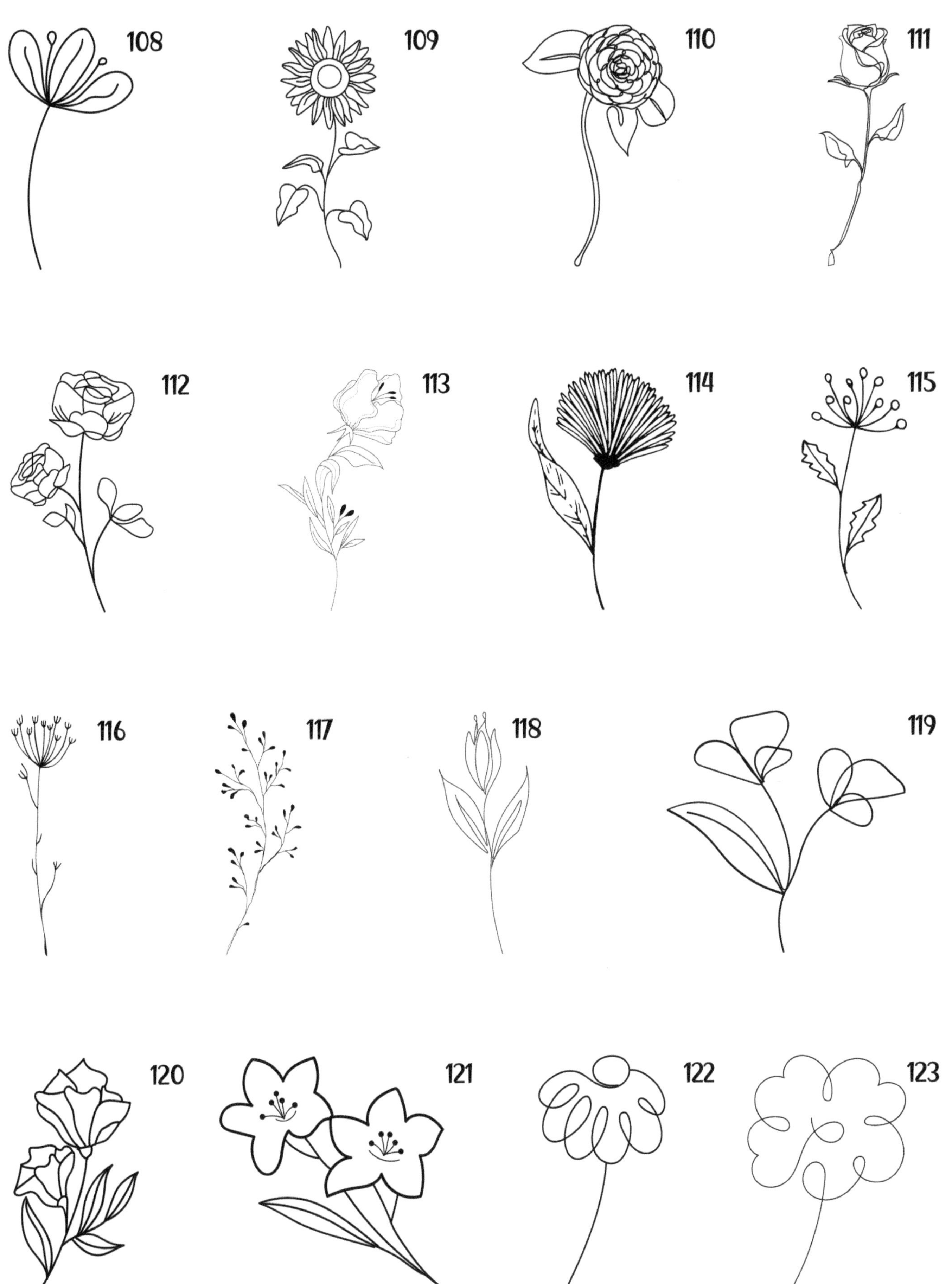
108
109
110
111
112
113
114
115
116
117
118
119
120
121
122
123

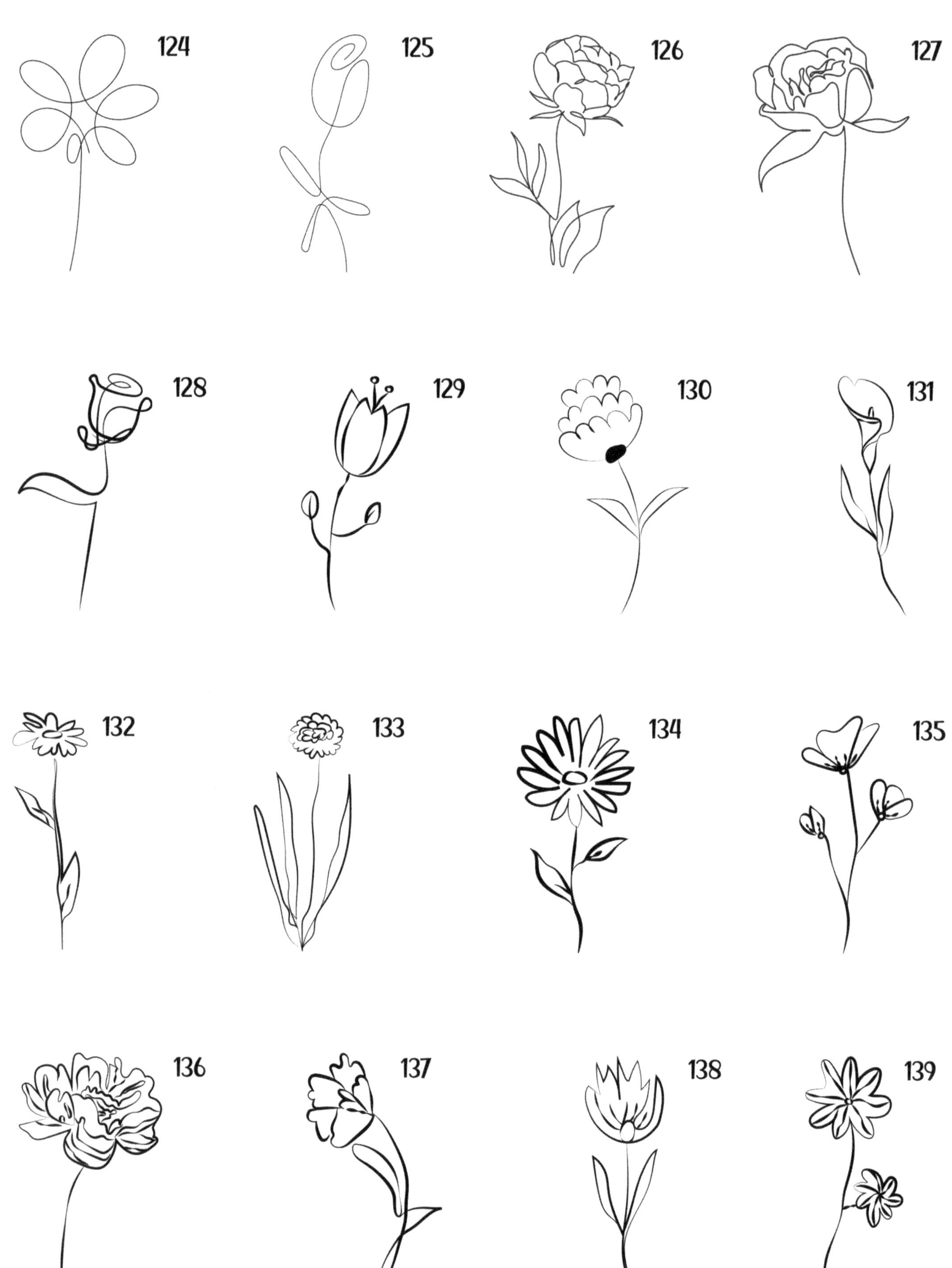

124
125
126
127
128
129
130
131
132
133
134
135
136
137
138
139

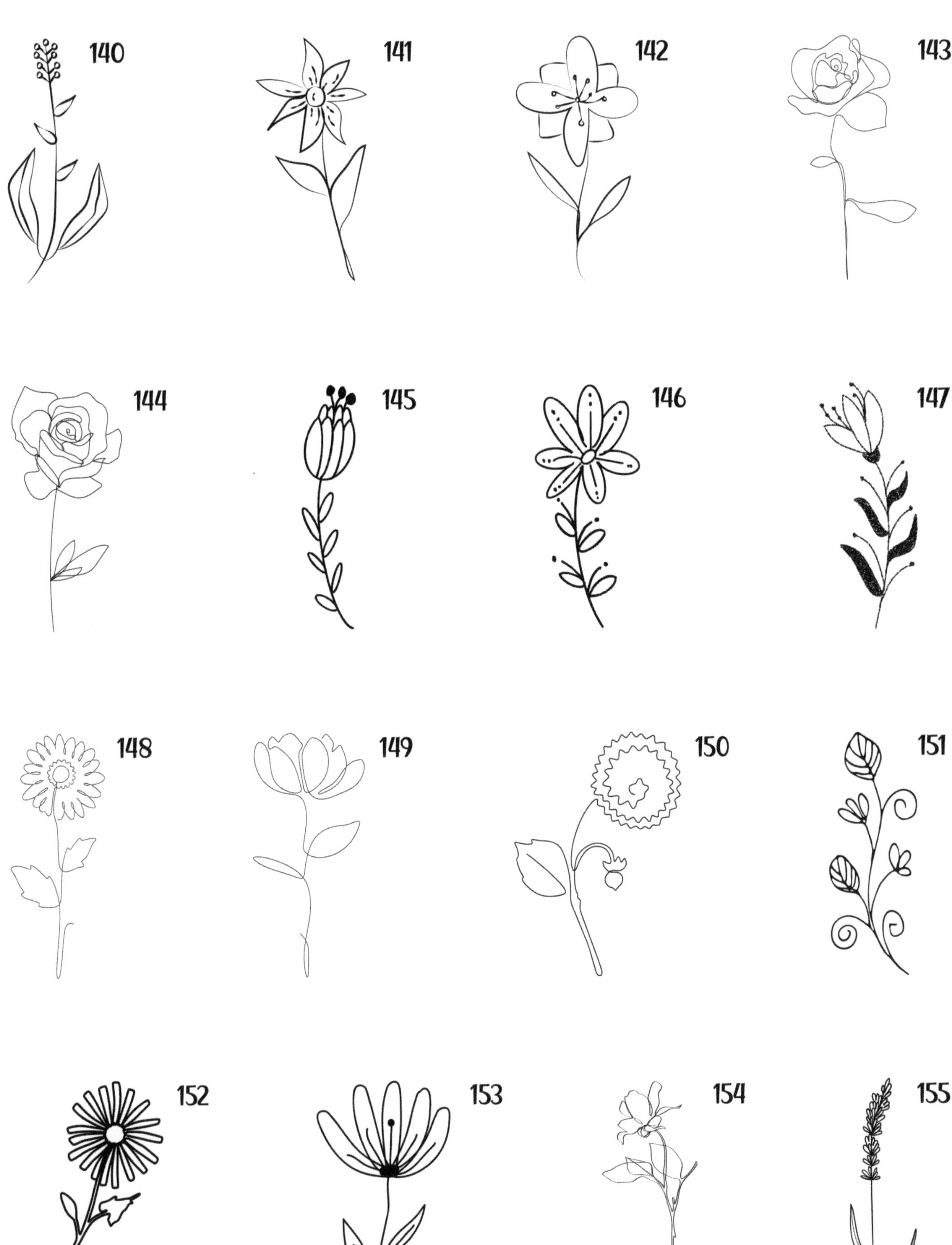

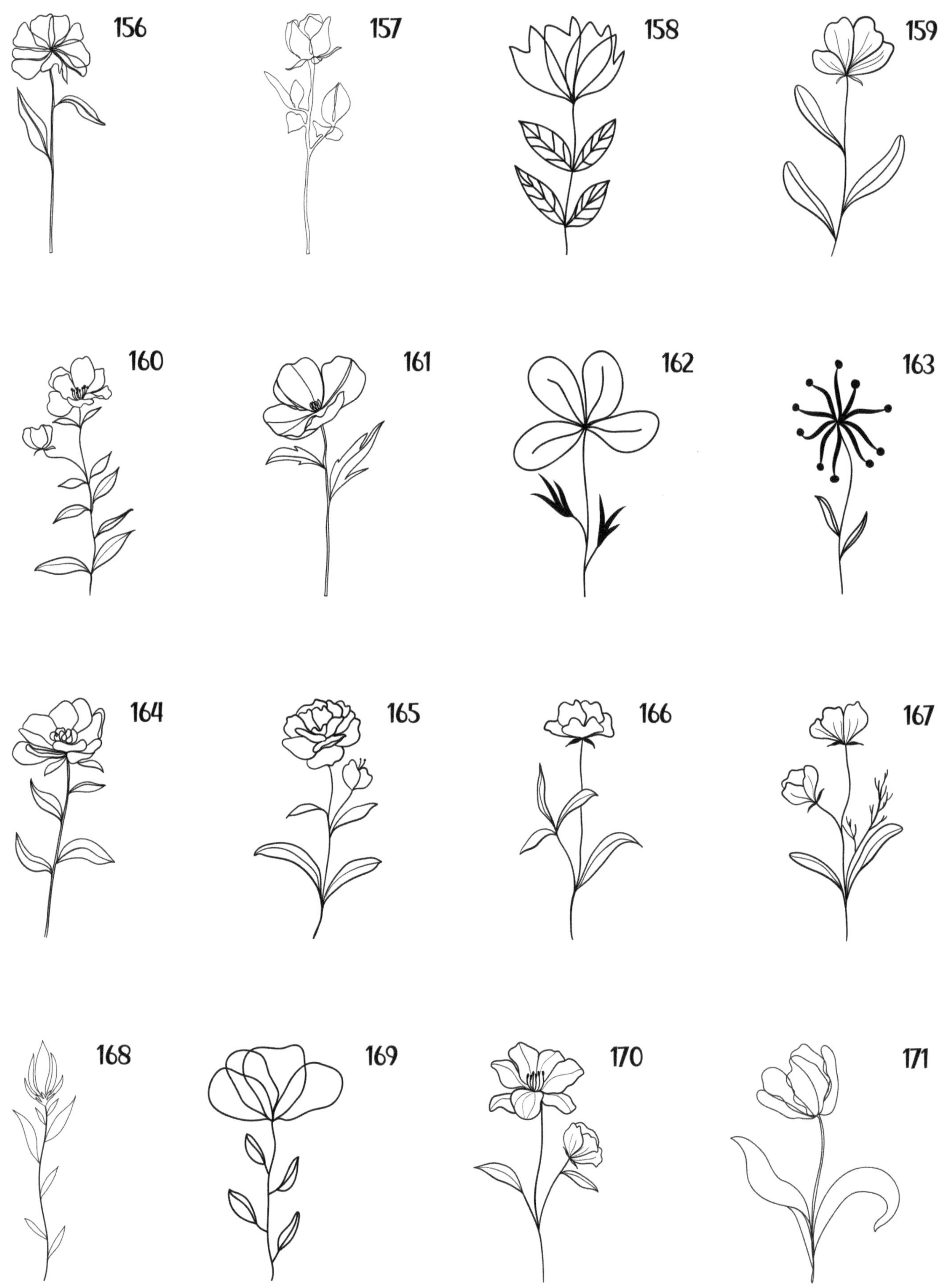

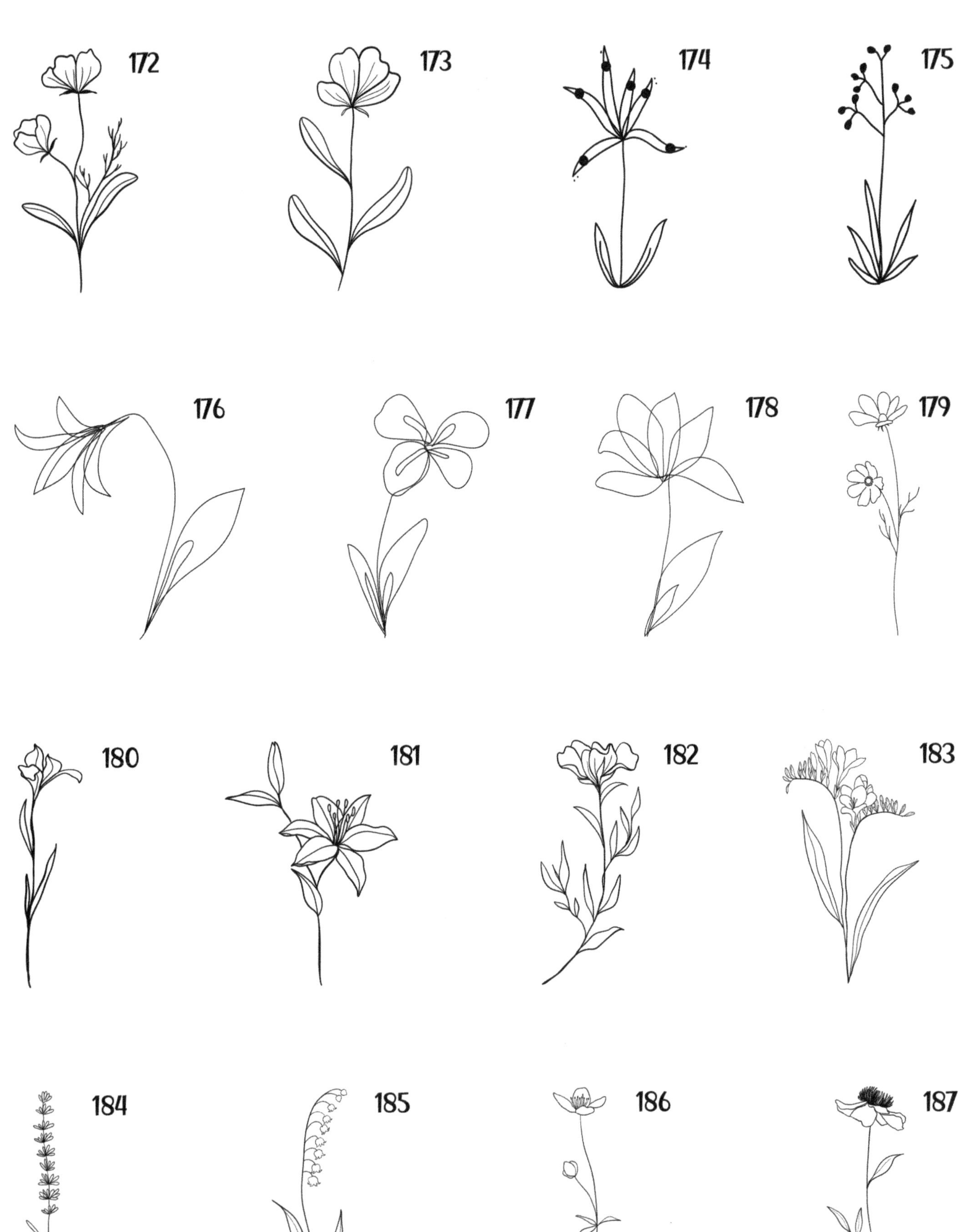

172
173
174
175
176
177
178
179
180
181
182
183
184
185
186
187

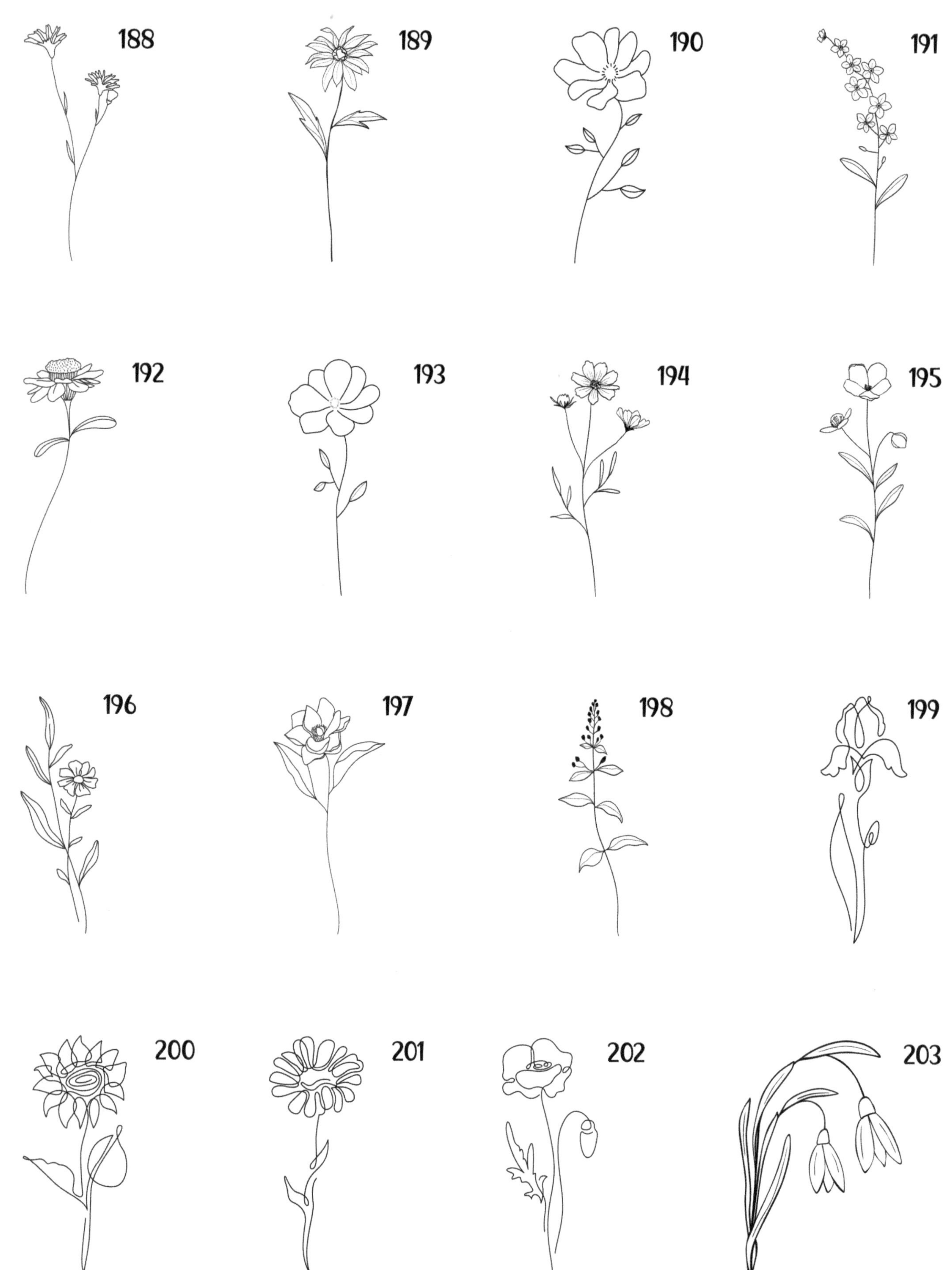

188
189
190
191
192
193
194
195
196
197
198
199
200
201
202
203

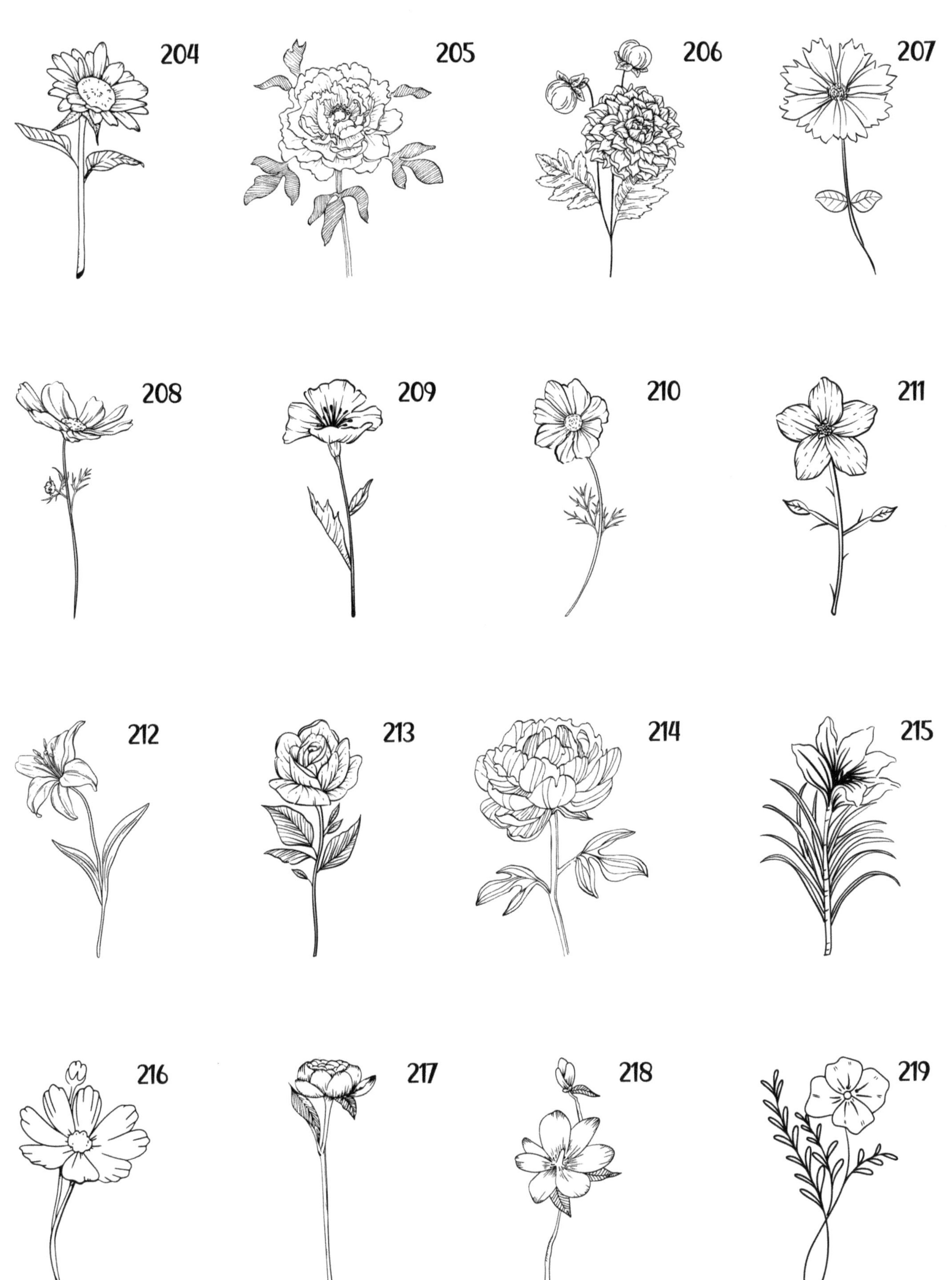

204
205
206
207
208
209
210
211
212
213
214
215
216
217
218
219

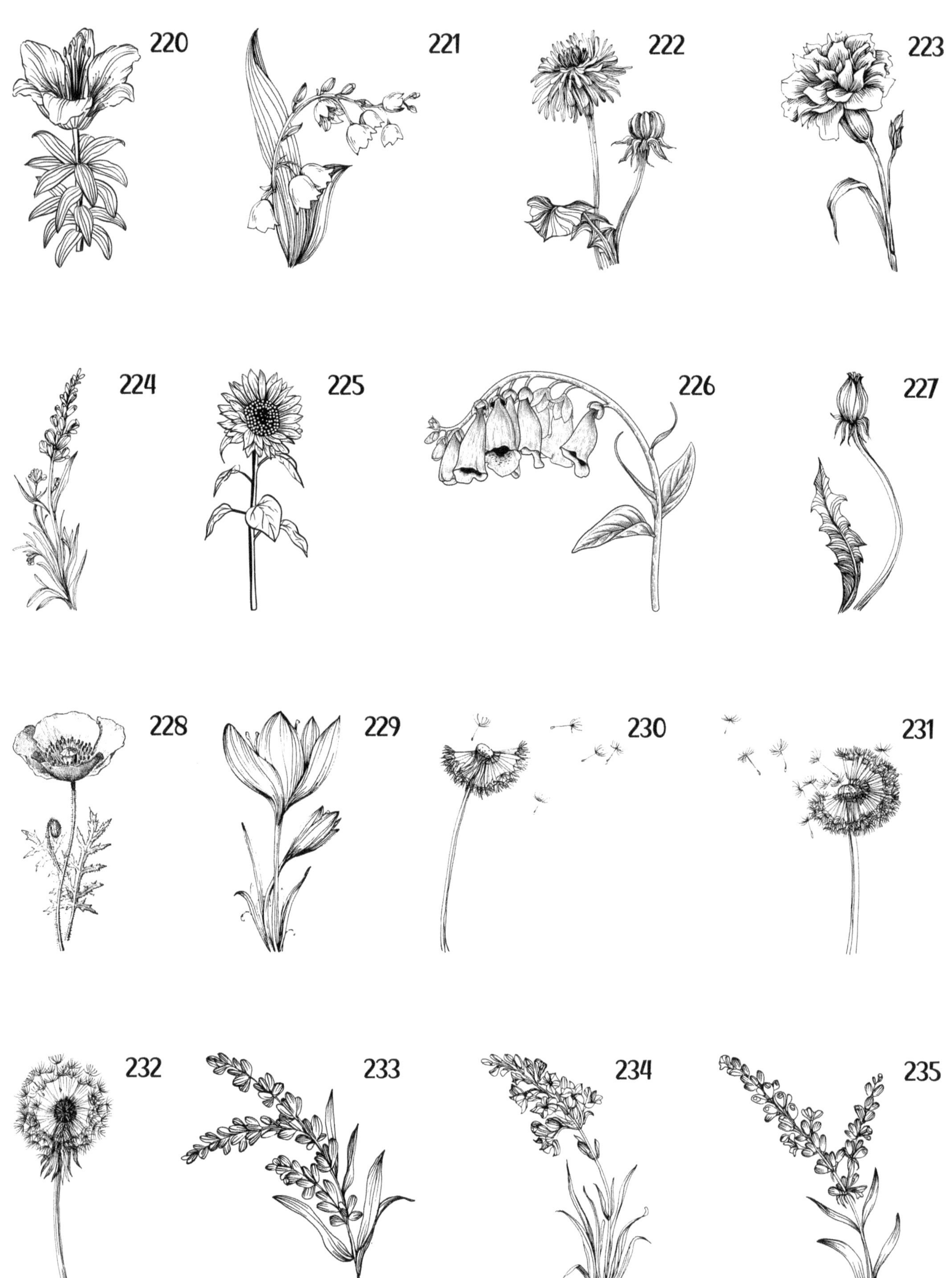

220
221
222
223
224
225
226
227
228
229
230
231
232
233
234
235

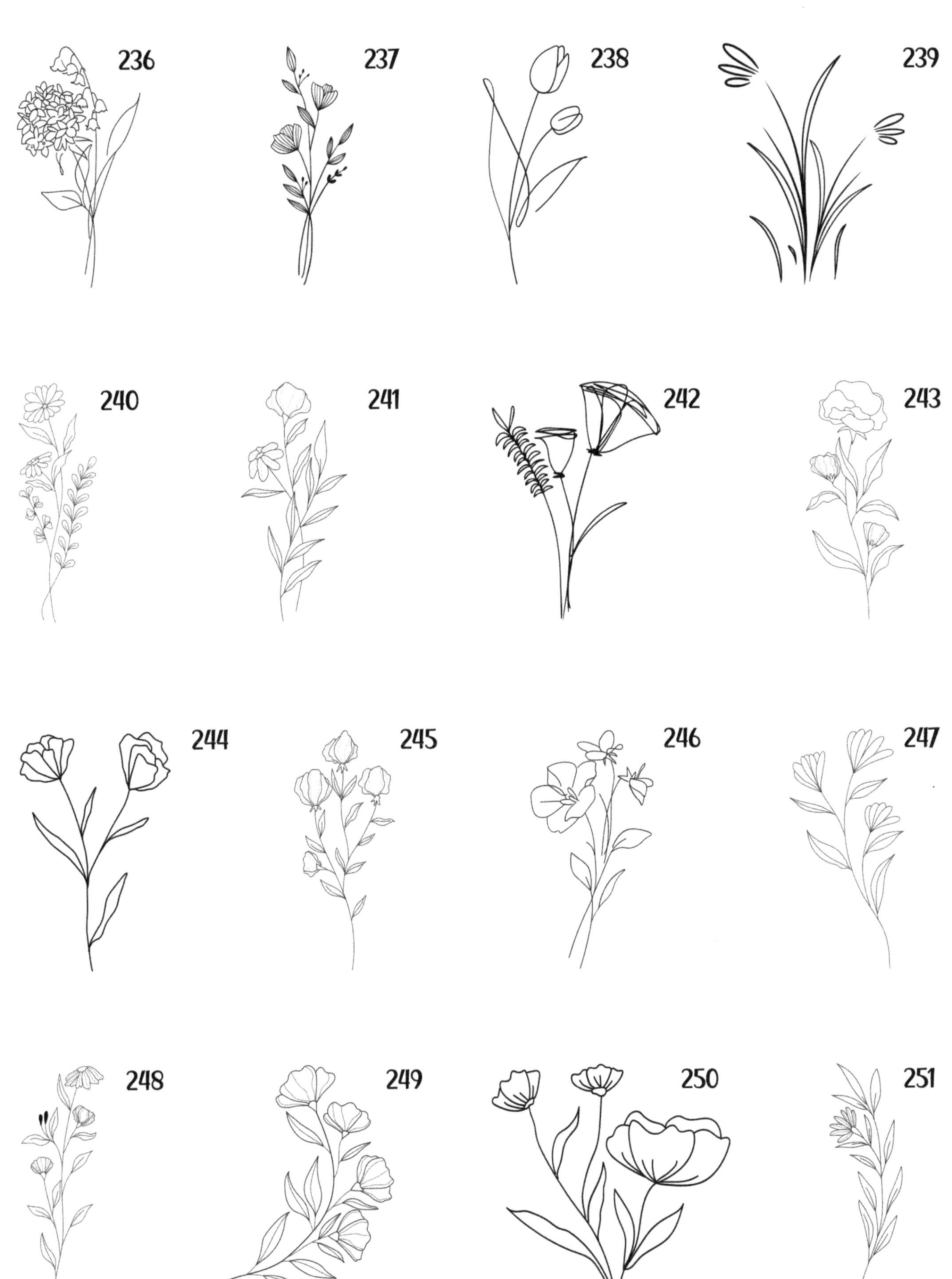

236
237
238
239
240
241
242
243
244
245
246
247
248
249
250
251

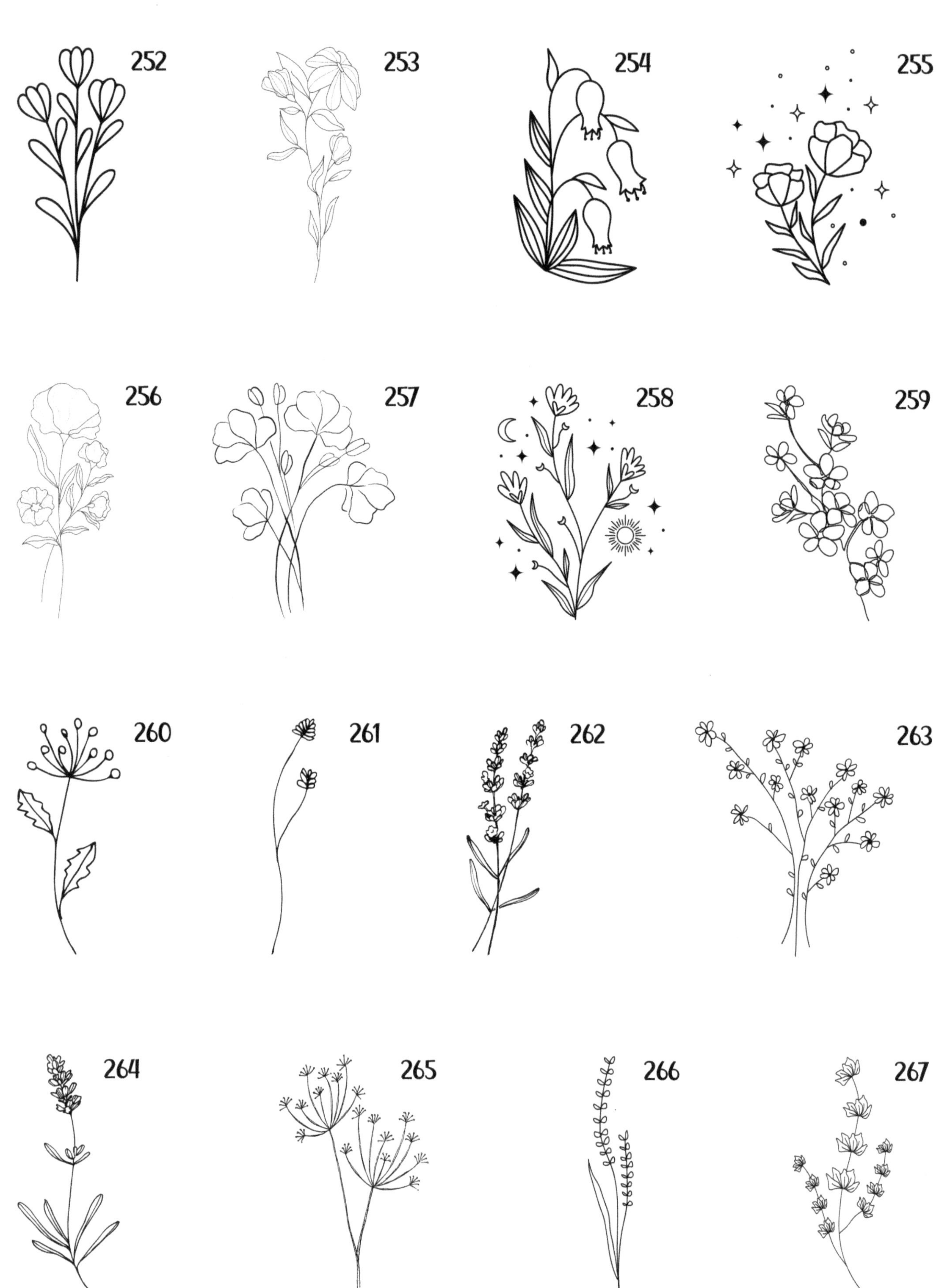

252
253
254
255
256
257
258
259
260
261
262
263
264
265
266
267

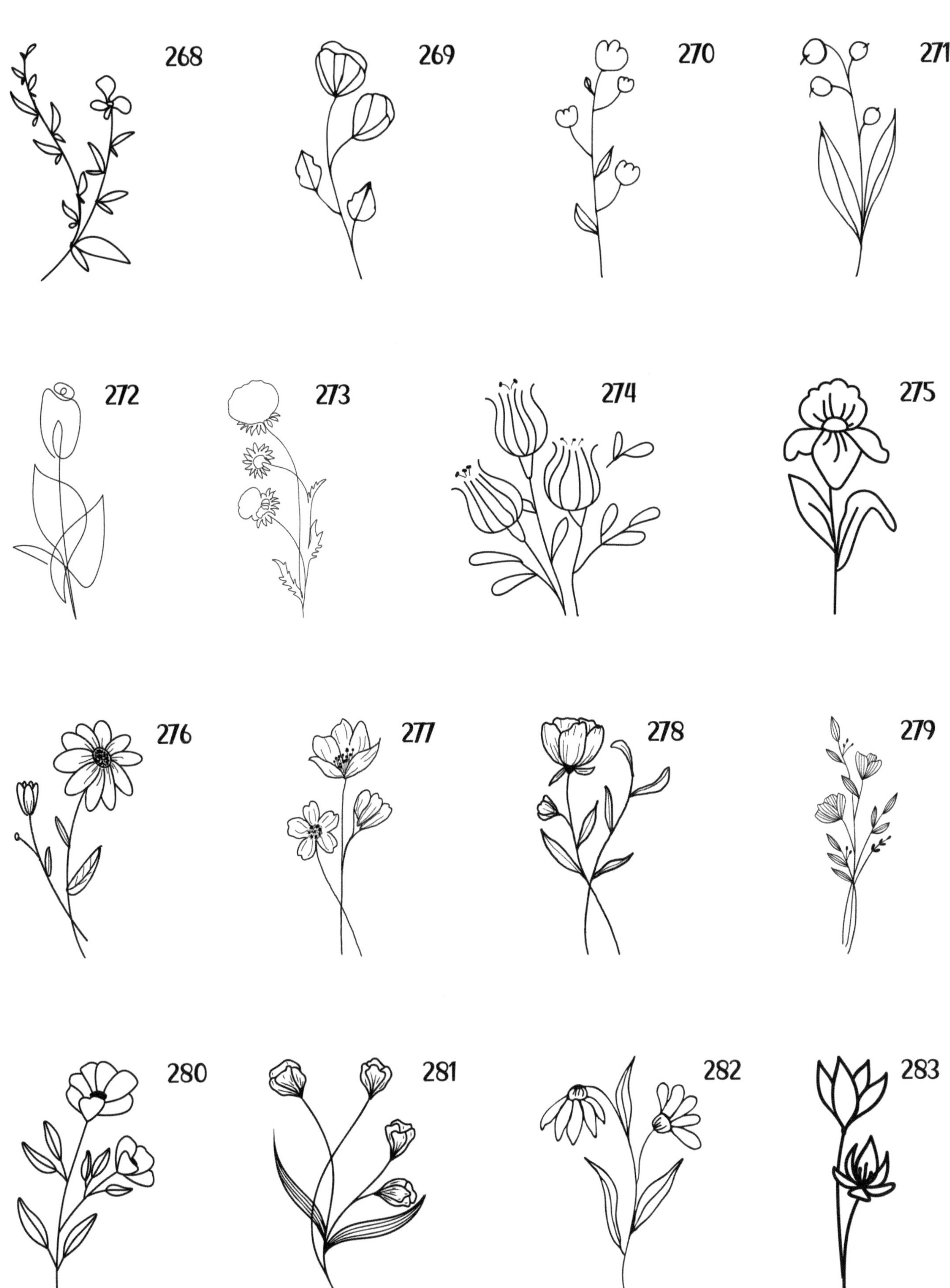
268
269
270
271
272
273
274
275
276
277
278
279
280
281
282
283

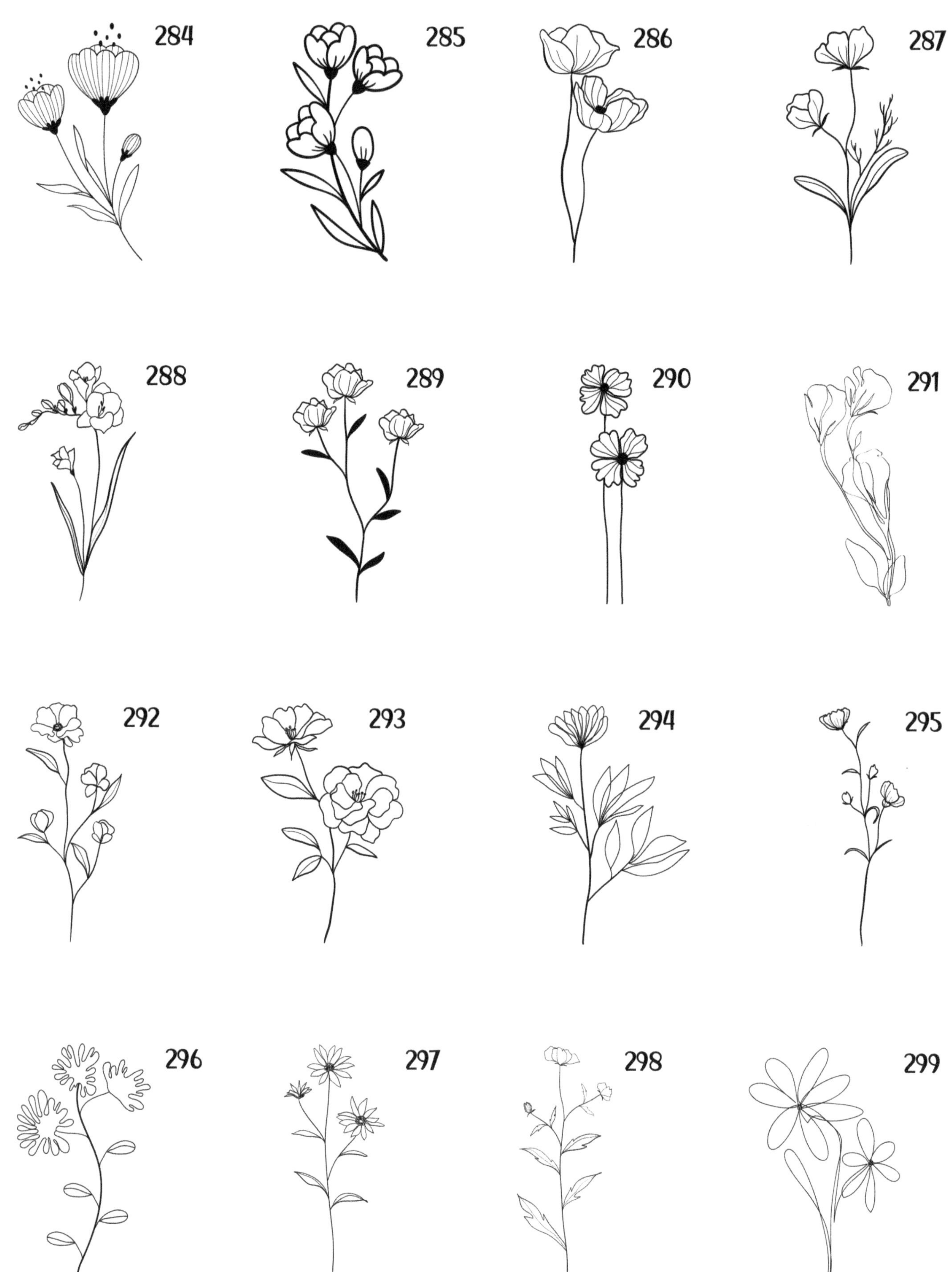

284
285
286
287
288
289
290
291
292
293
294
295
296
297
298
299

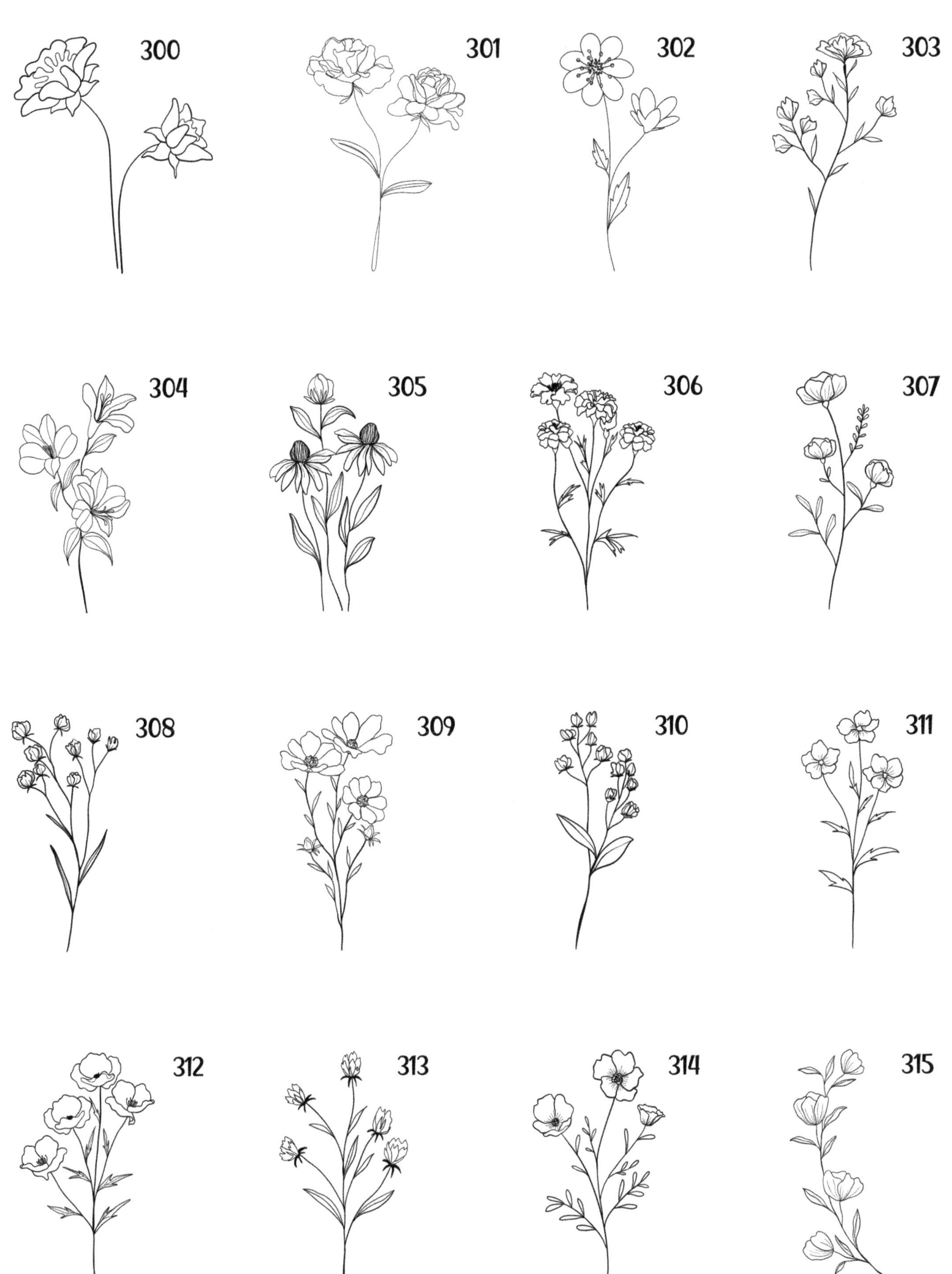

300
301
302
303
304
305
306
307
308
309
310
311
312
313
314
315

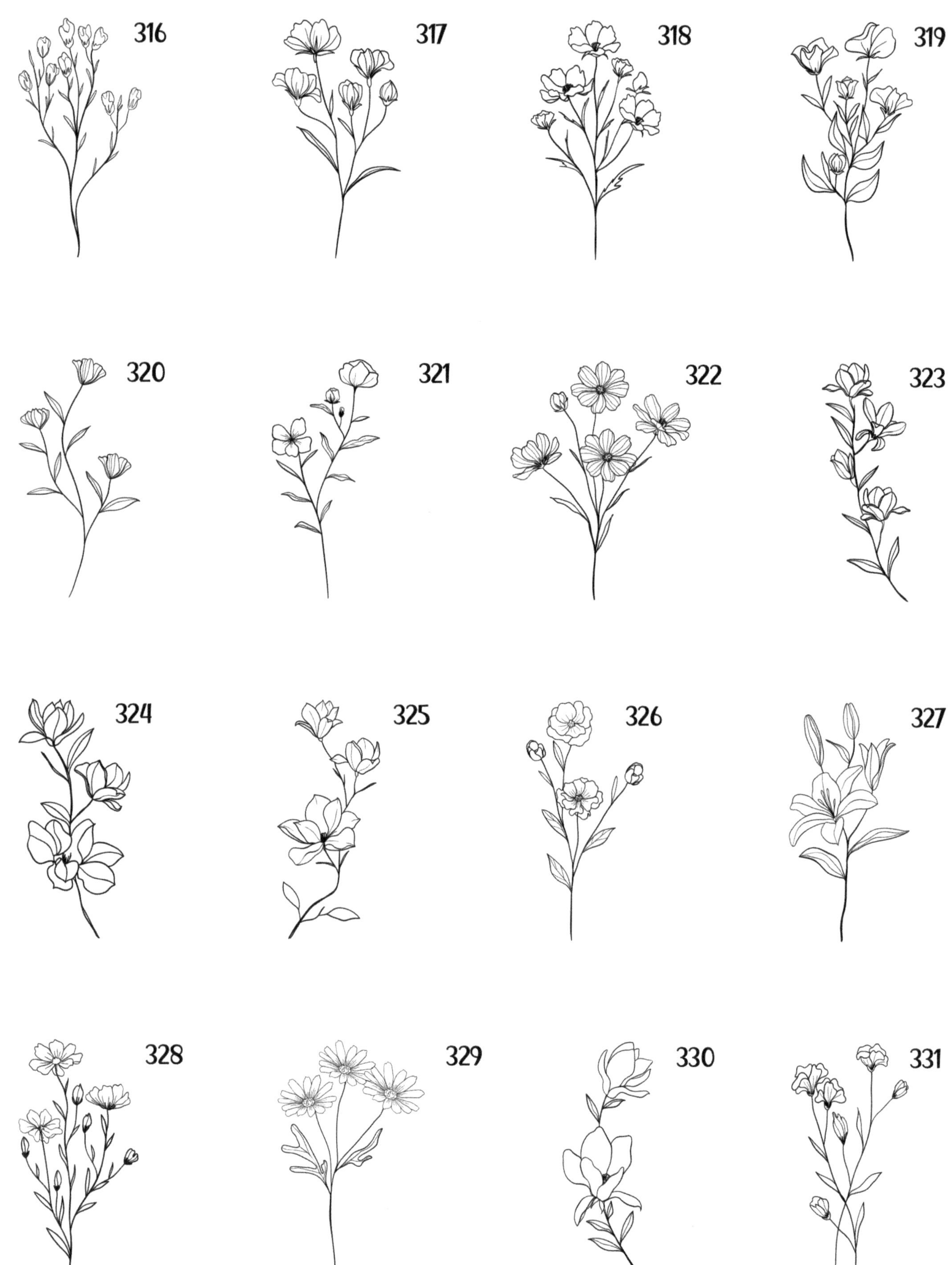

316
317
318
319
320
321
322
323
324
325
326
327
328
329
330
331

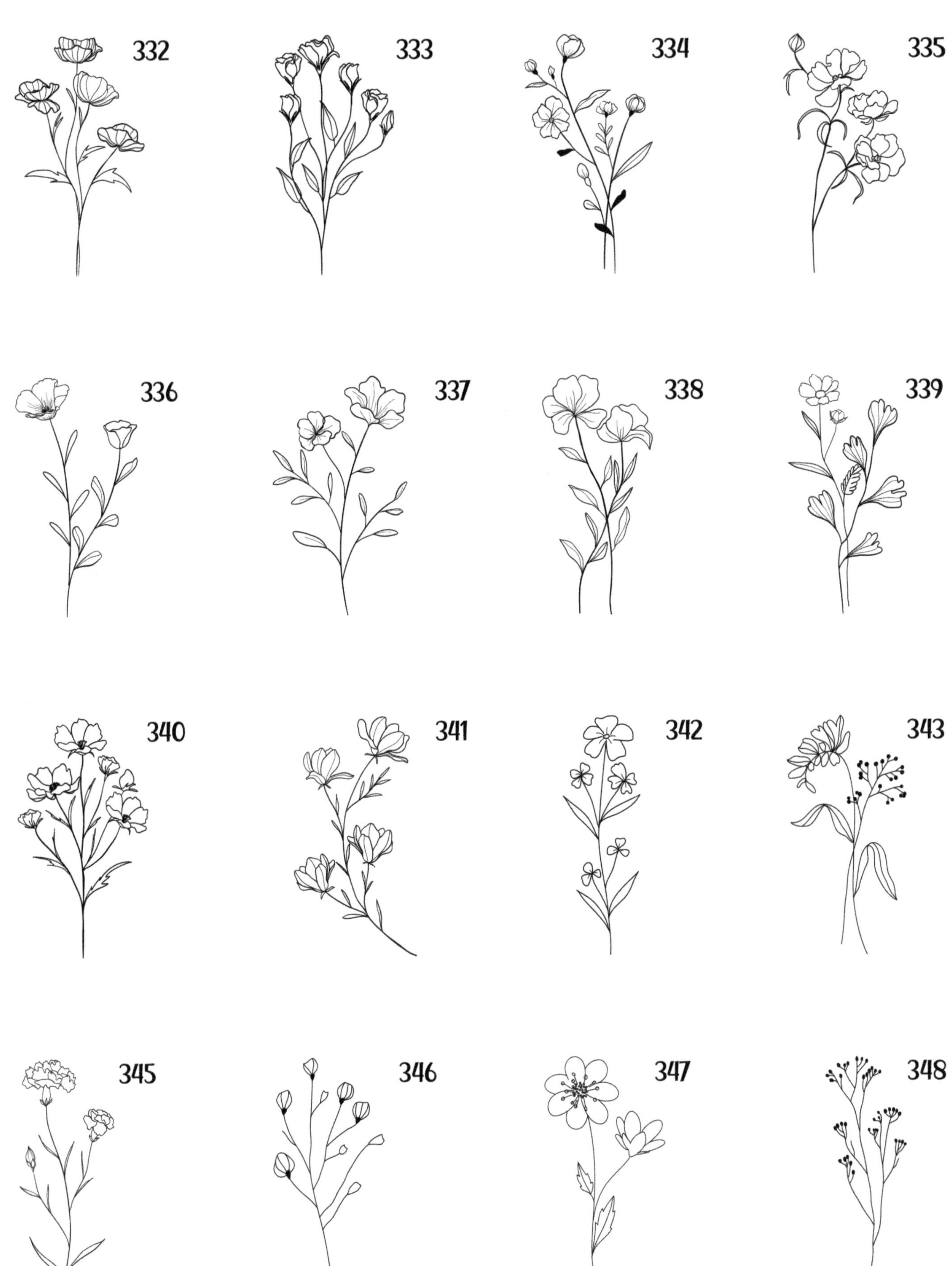

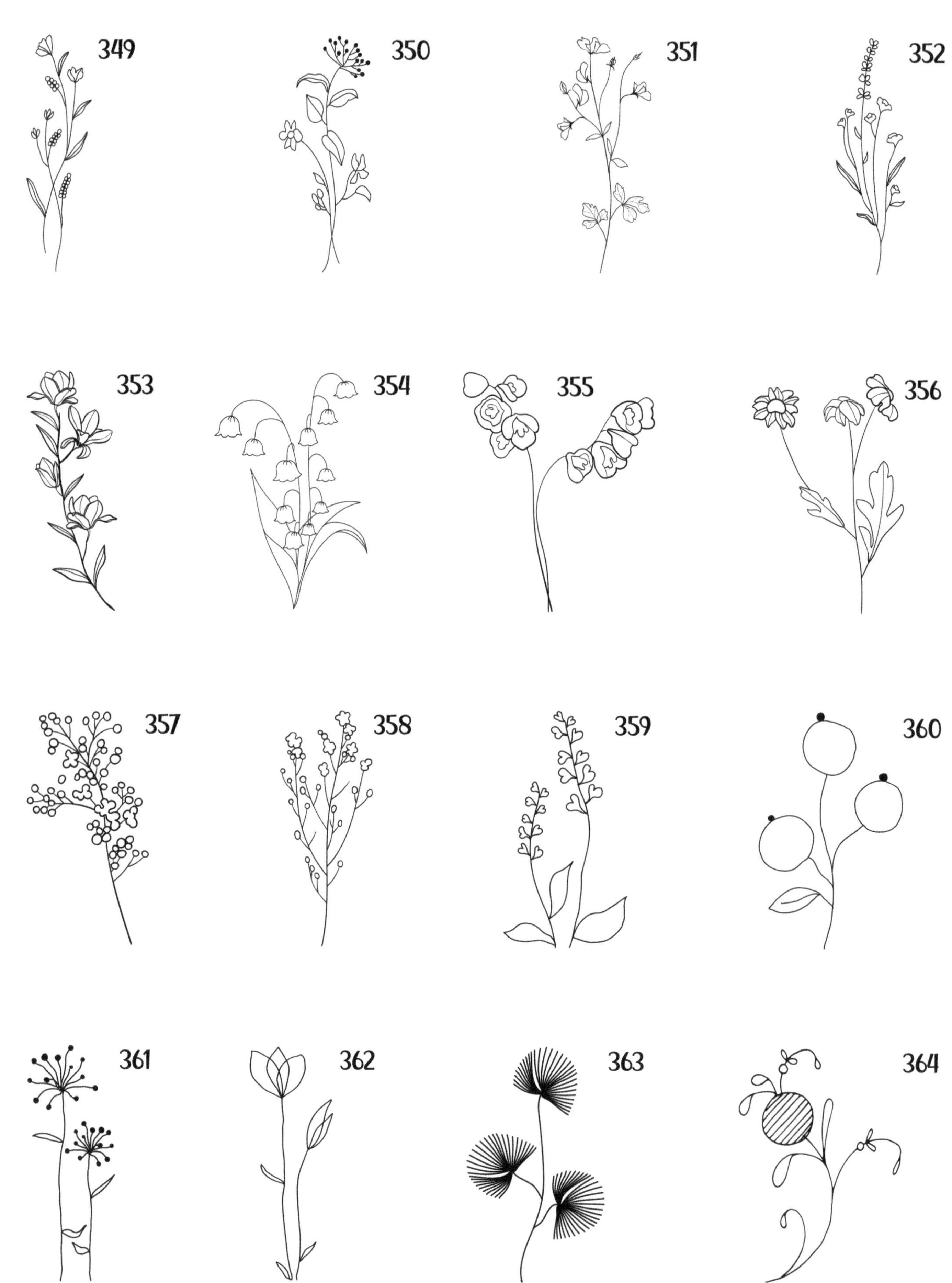

349
350
351
352
353
354
355
356
357
358
359
360
361
362
363
364

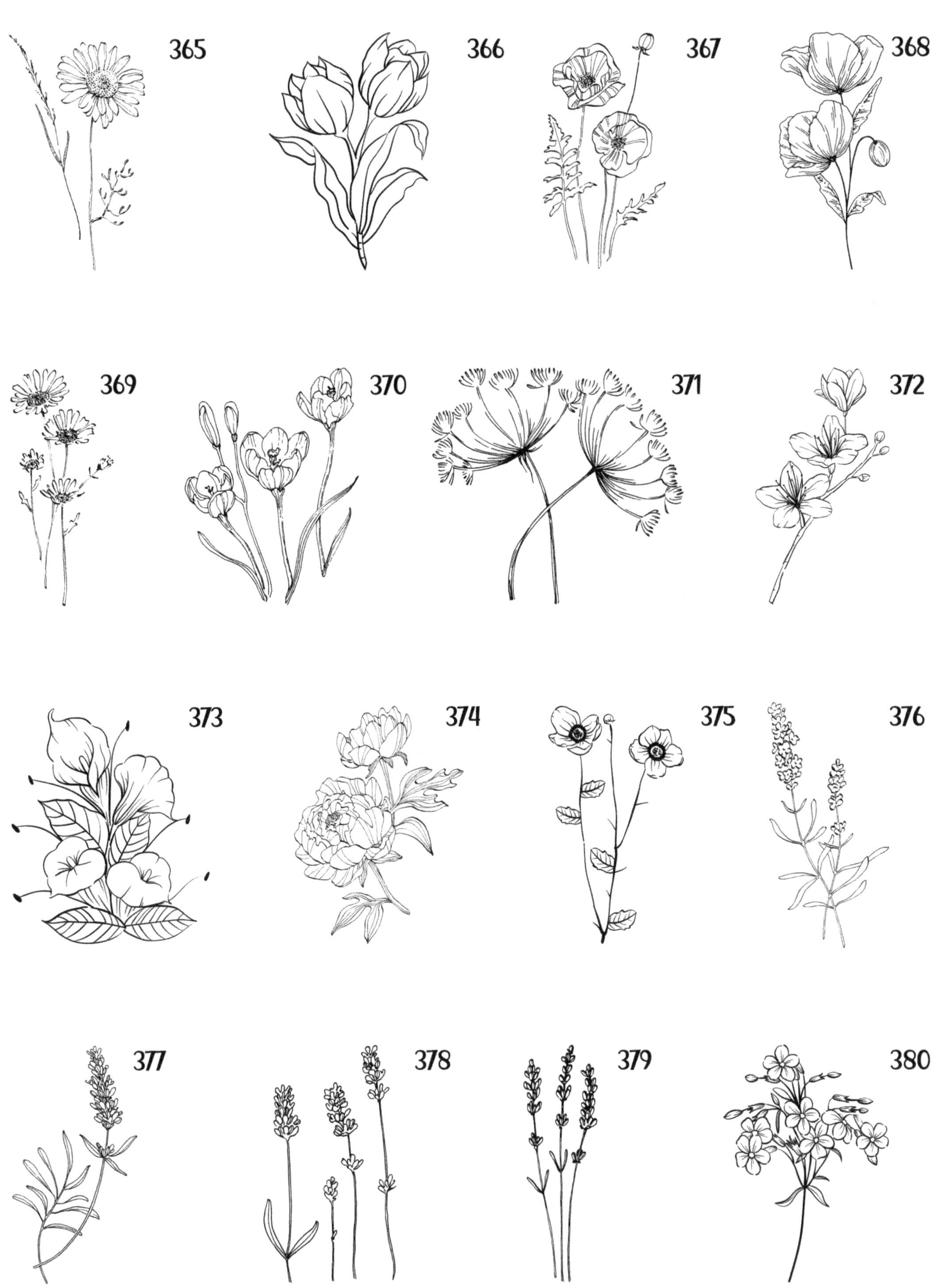

365
366
367
368
369
370
371
372
373
374
375
376
377
378
379
380

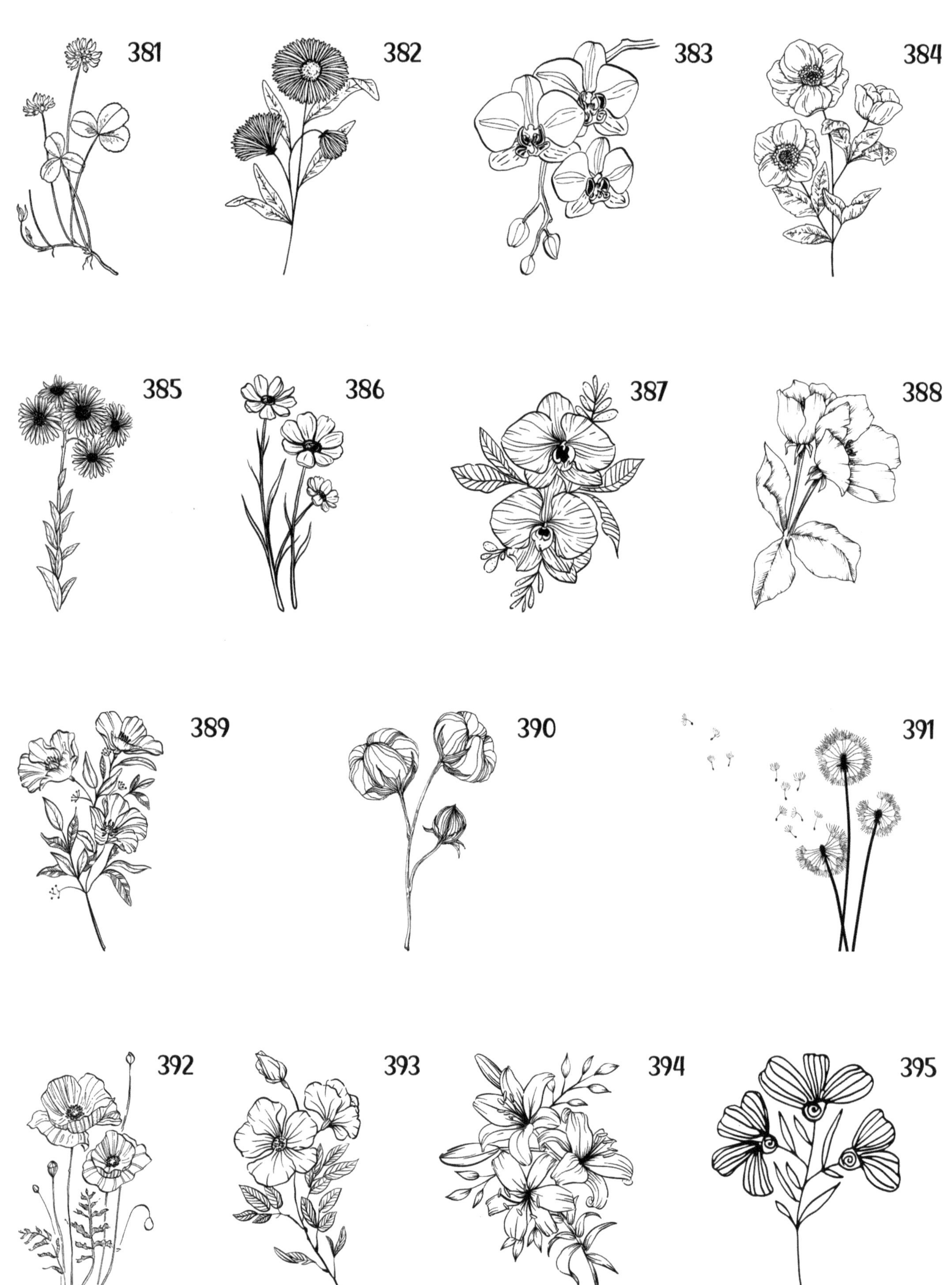

381
382
383
384
385
386
387
388
389
390
391
392
393
394
395

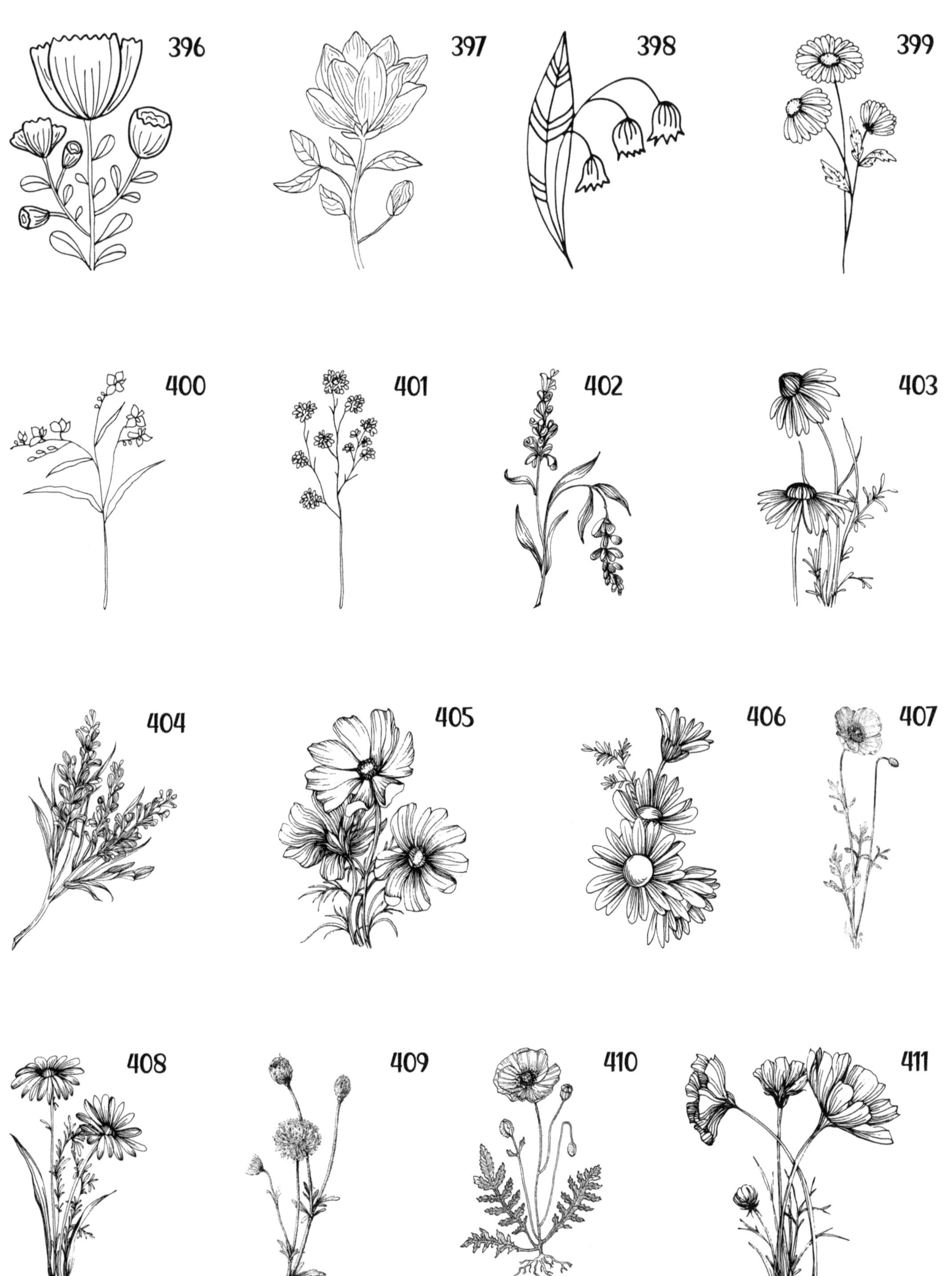
396
397
398
399
400
401
402
403
404
405
406
407
408
409
410
411

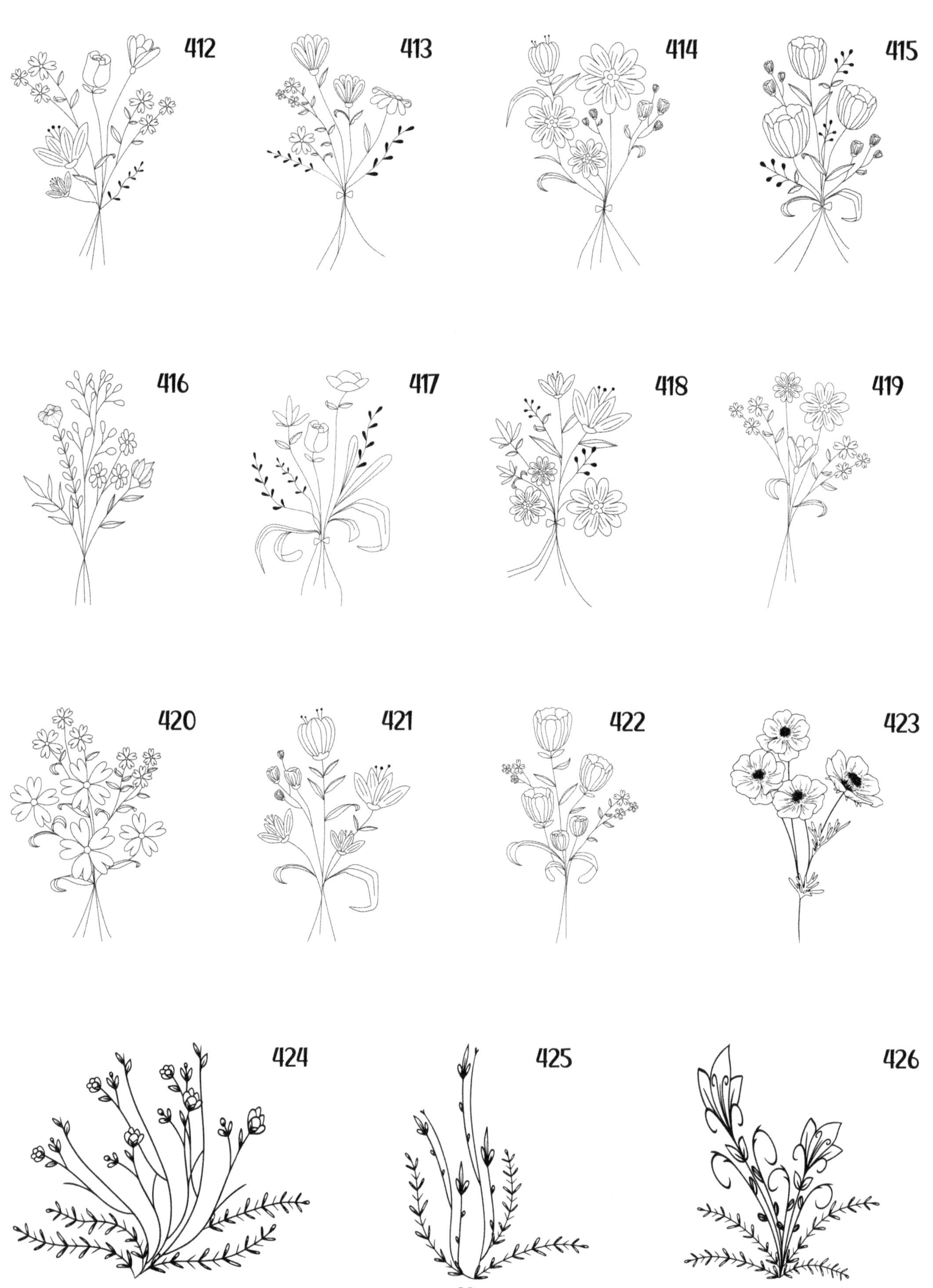
412
413
414
415
416
417
418
419
420
421
422
423
424
425
426

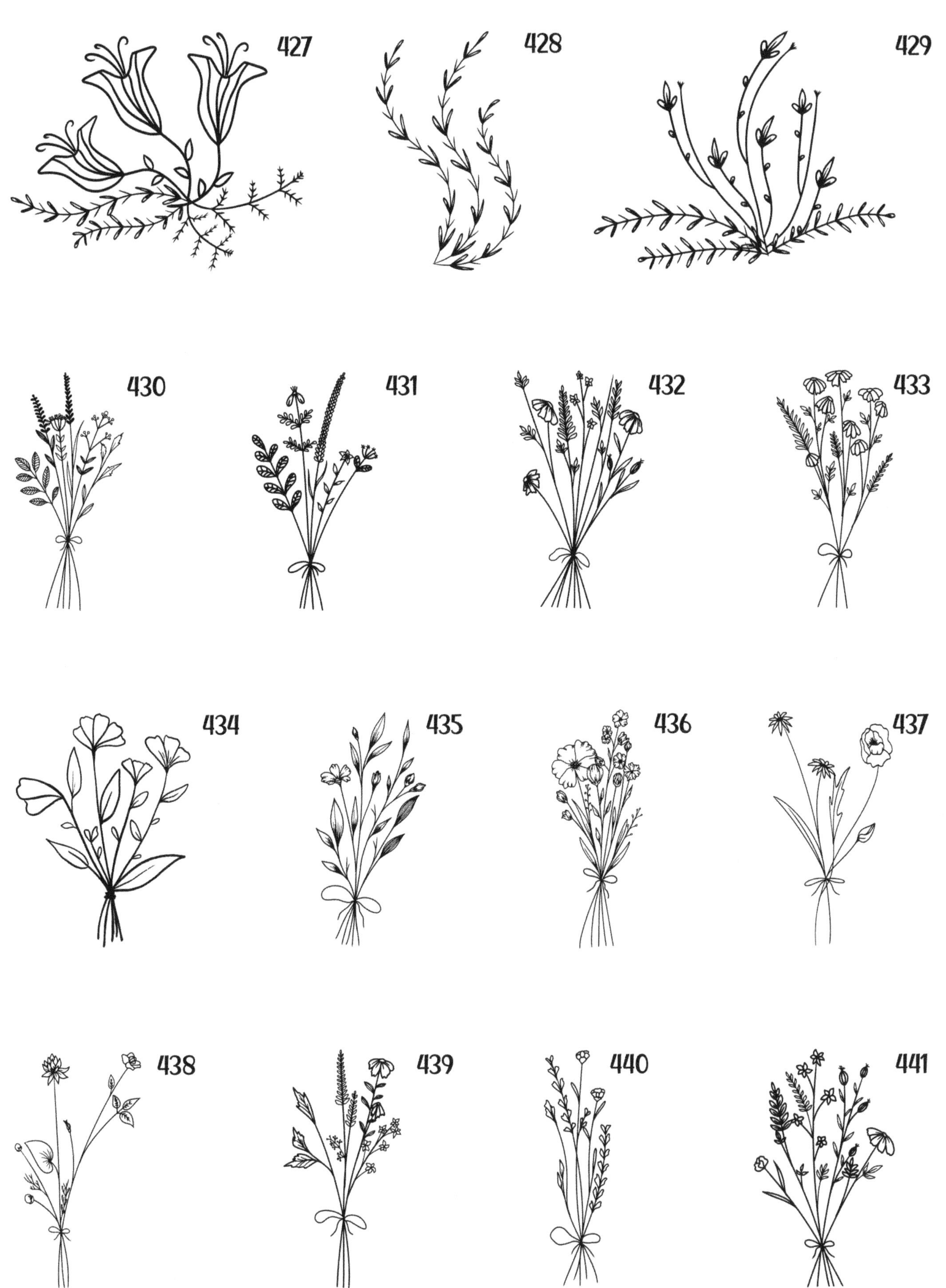

427
428
429
430
431
432
433
434
435
436
437
438
439
440
441

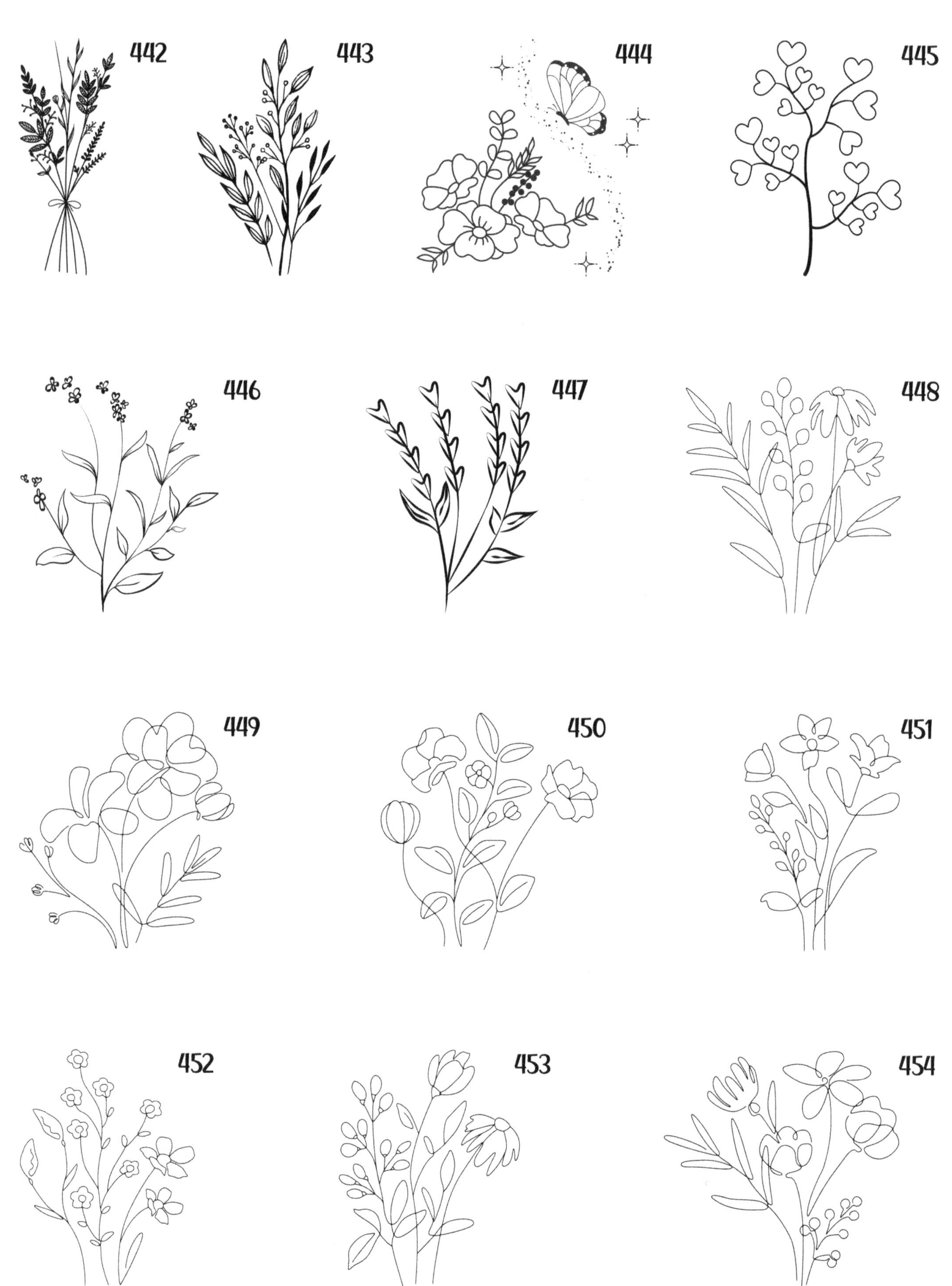

442
443
444
445
446
447
448
449
450
451
452
453
454

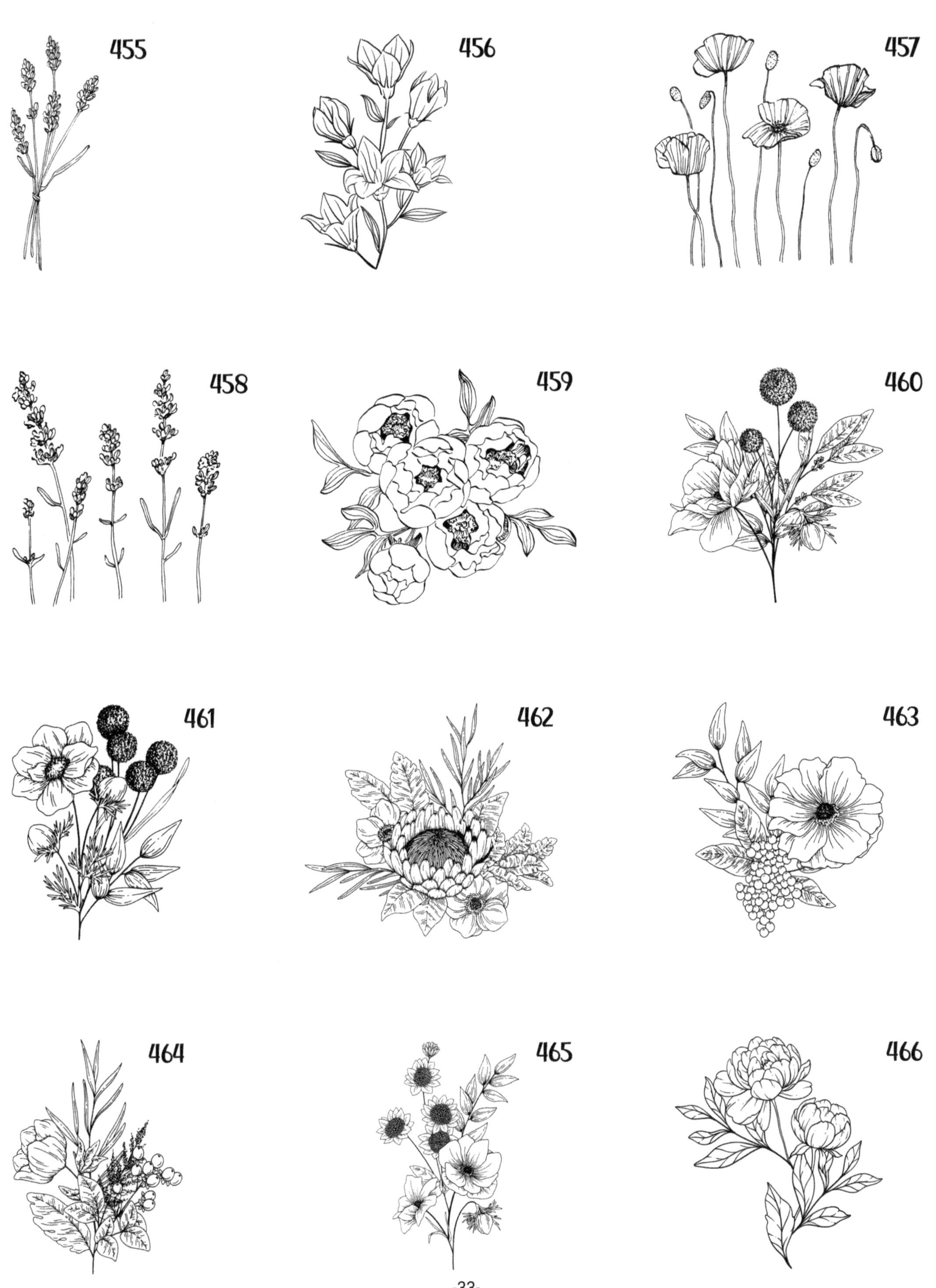

455
456
457
458
459
460
461
462
463
464
465
466

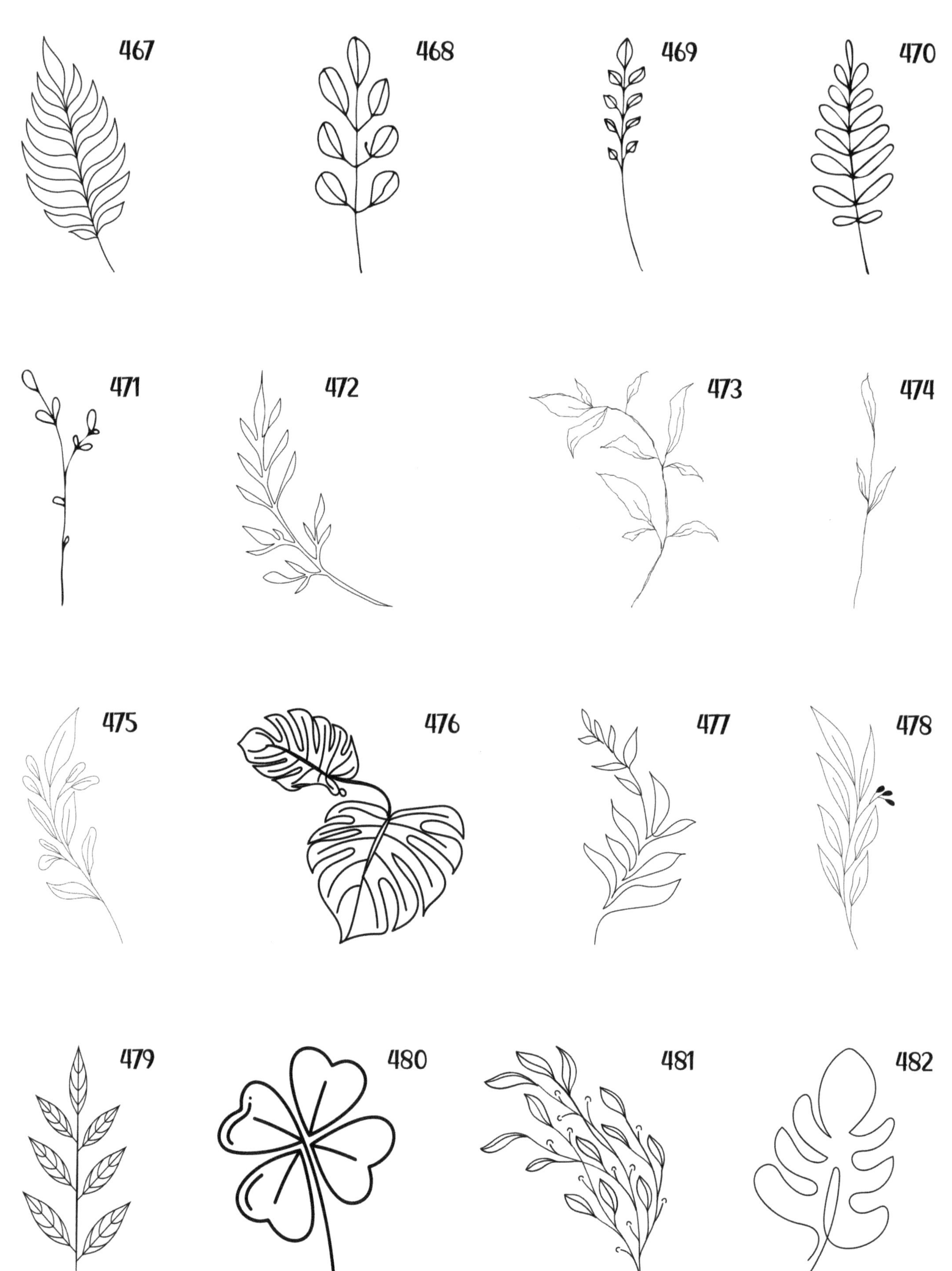

467
468
469
470
471
472
473
474
475
476
477
478
479
480
481
482

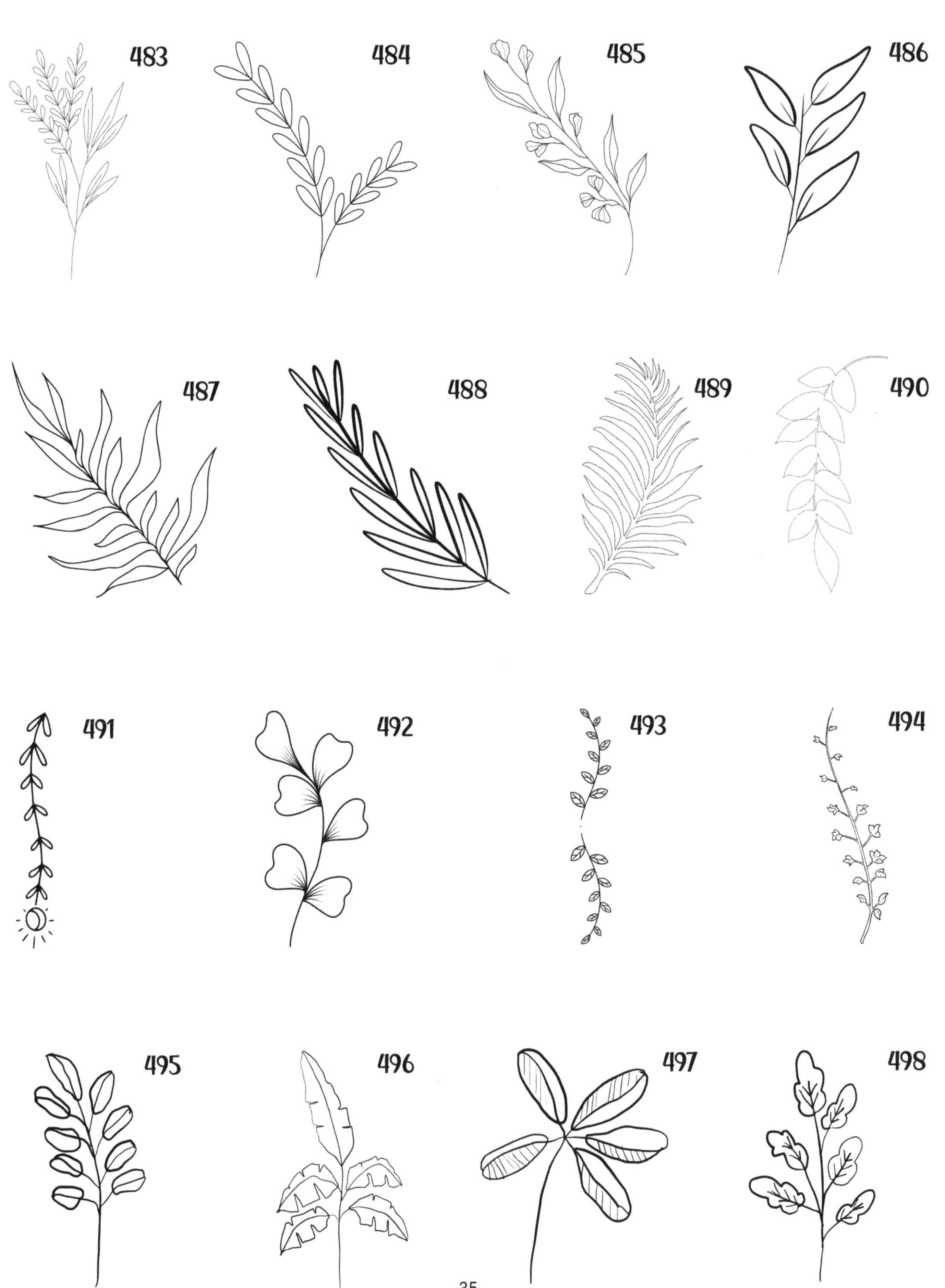

483
484
485
486
487
488
489
490
491
492
493
494
495
496
497
498

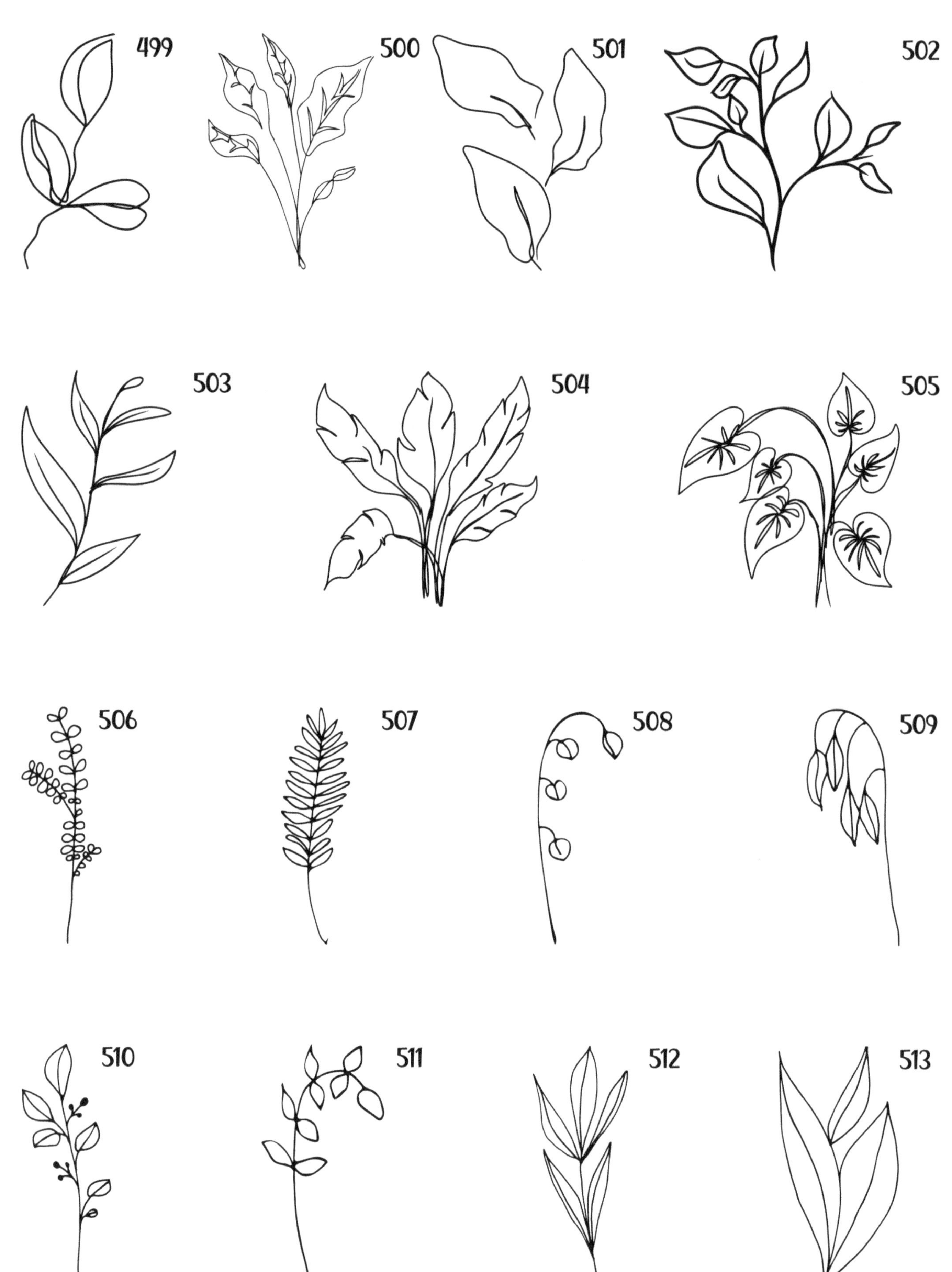

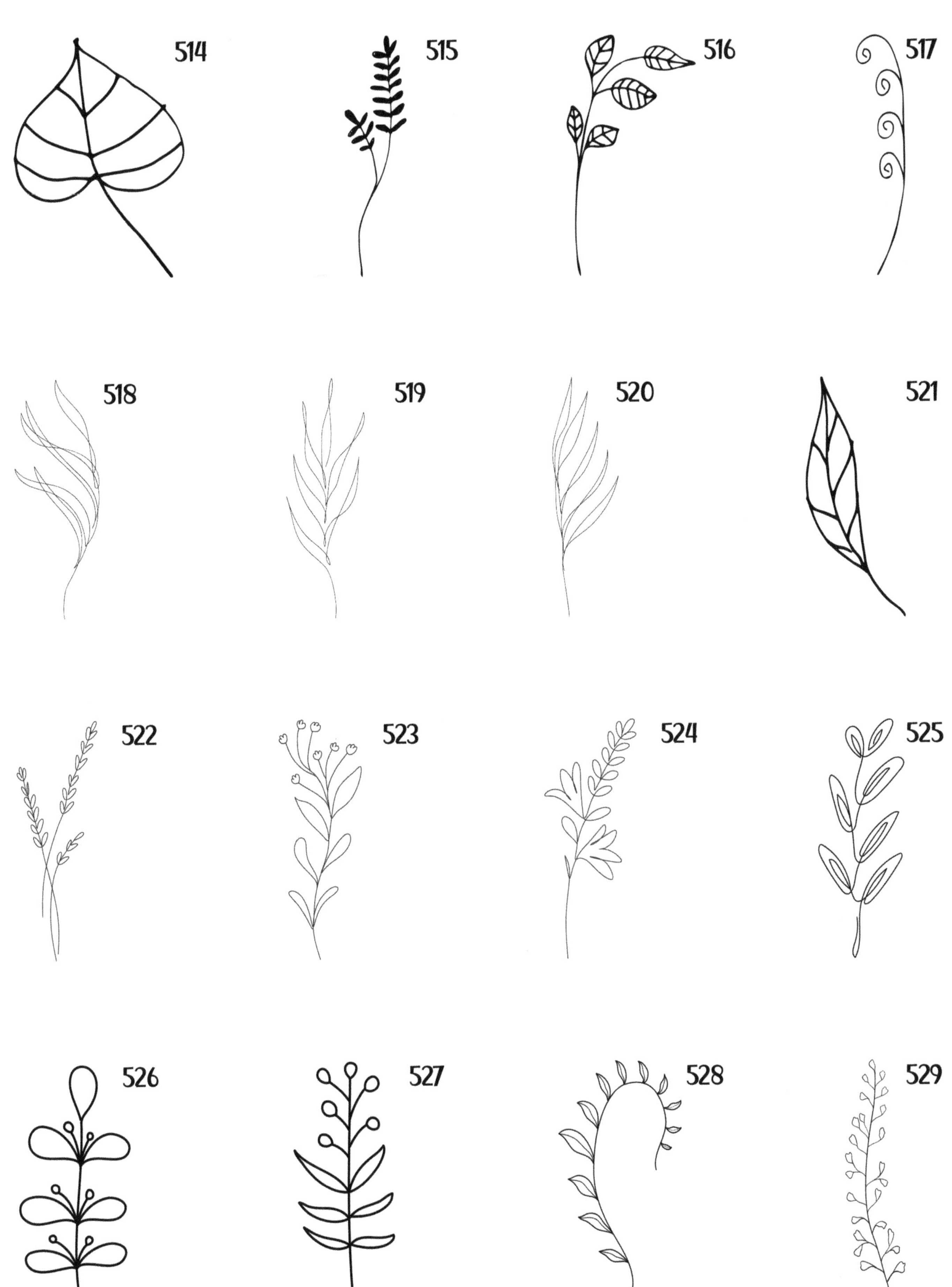

514
515
516
517
518
519
520
521
522
523
524
525
526
527
528
529

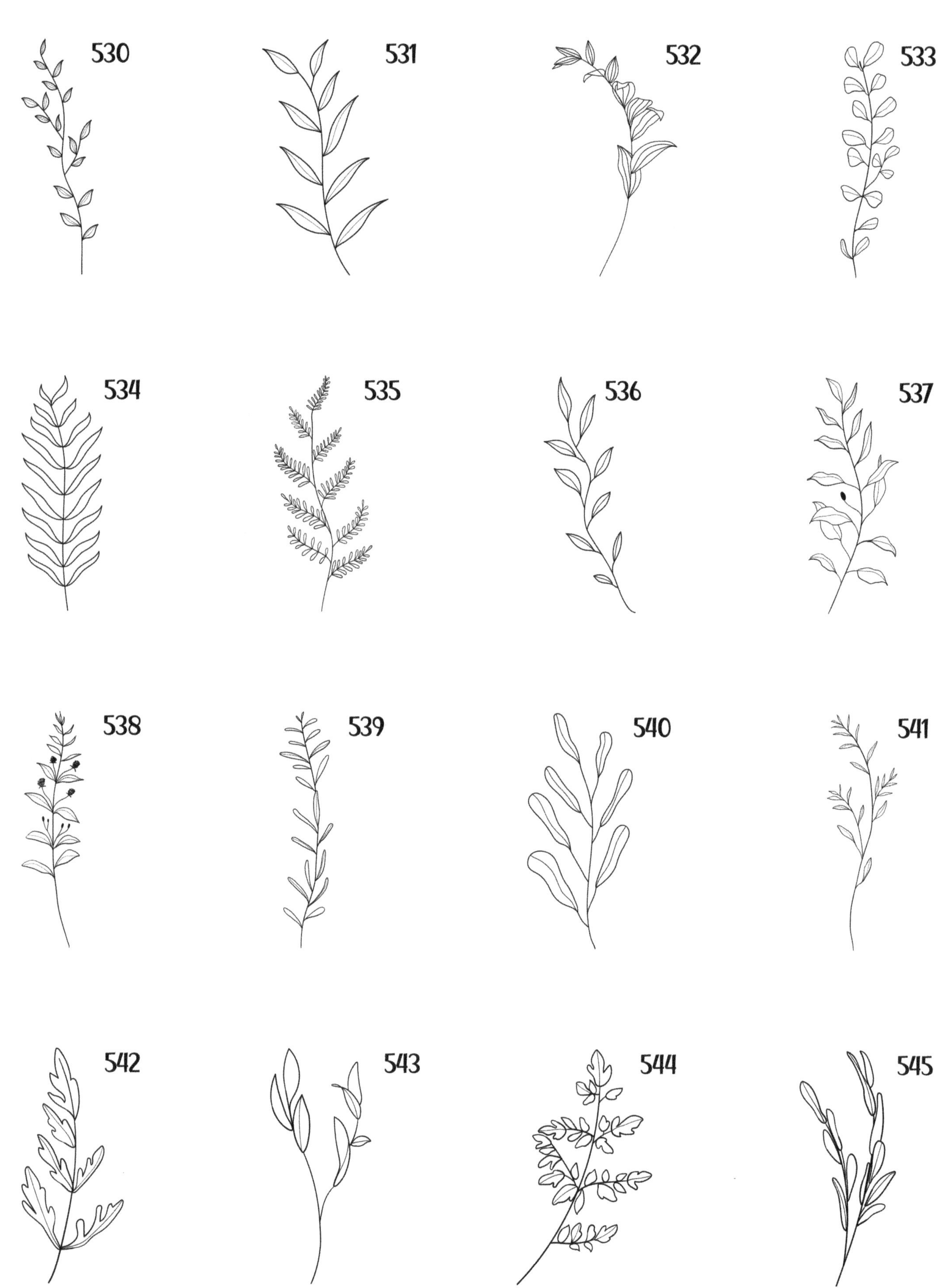

530
531
532
533
534
535
536
537
538
539
540
541
542
543
544
545

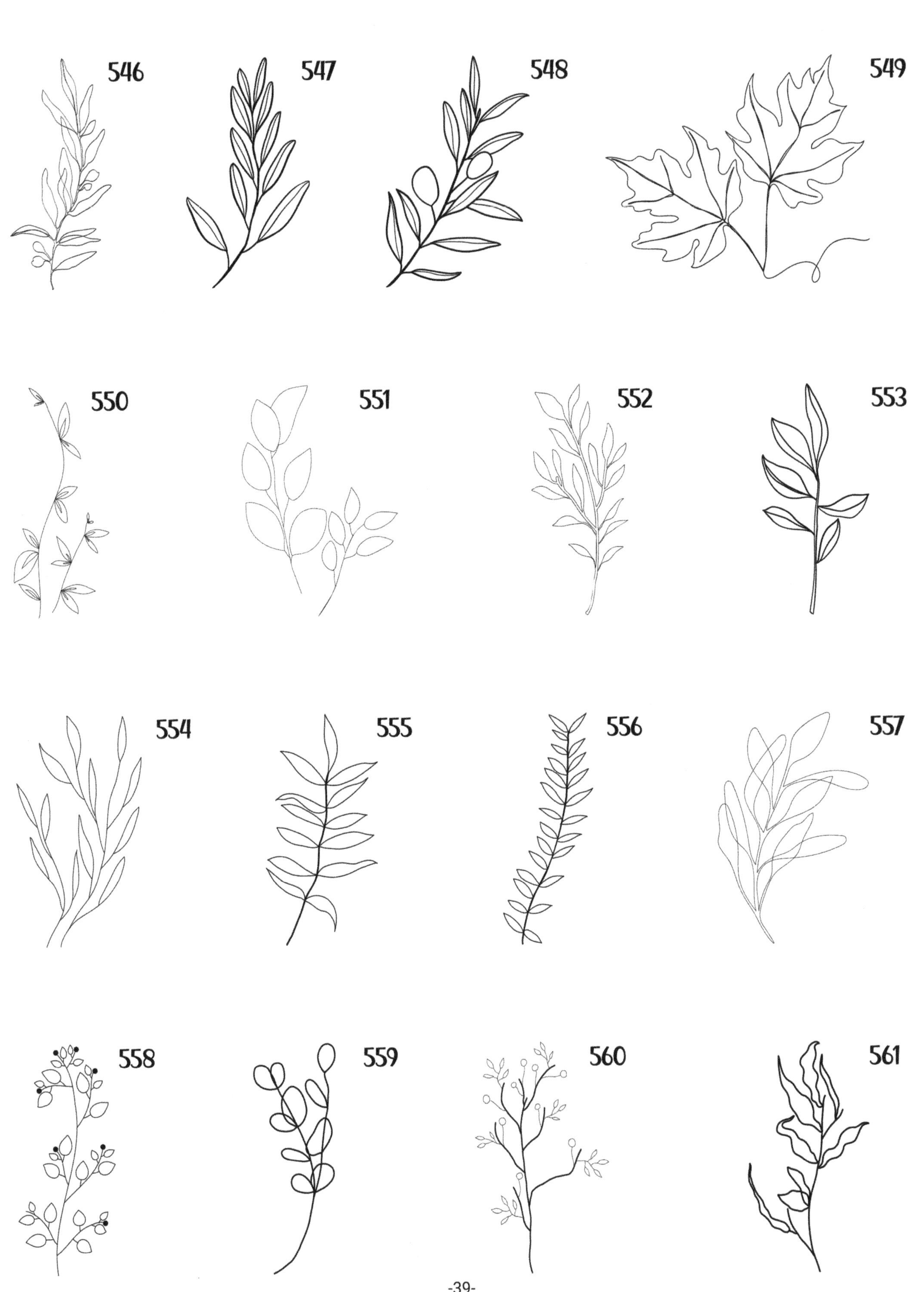

546
547
548
549
550
551
552
553
554
555
556
557
558
559
560
561

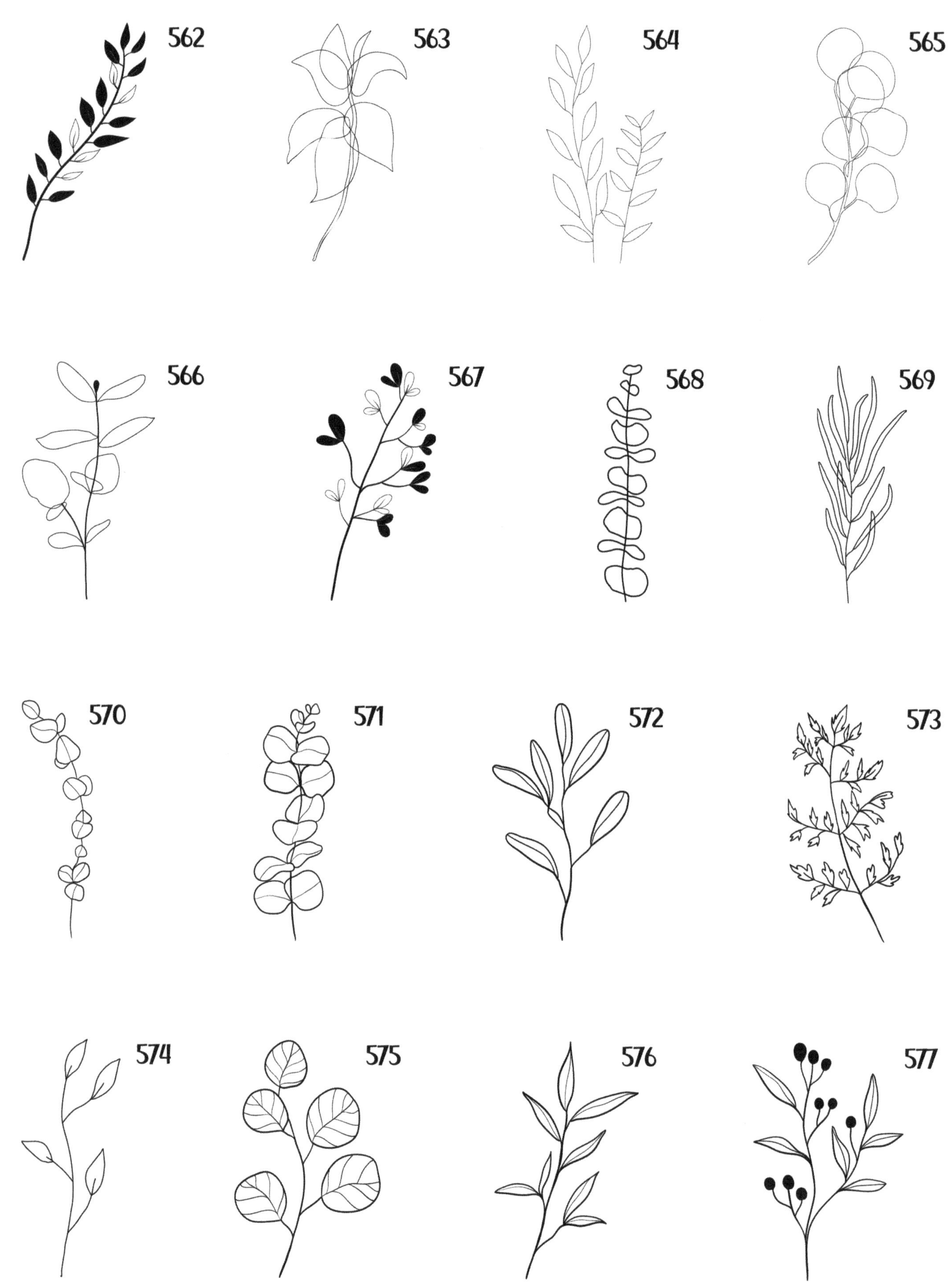

562
563
564
565
566
567
568
569
570
571
572
573
574
575
576
577

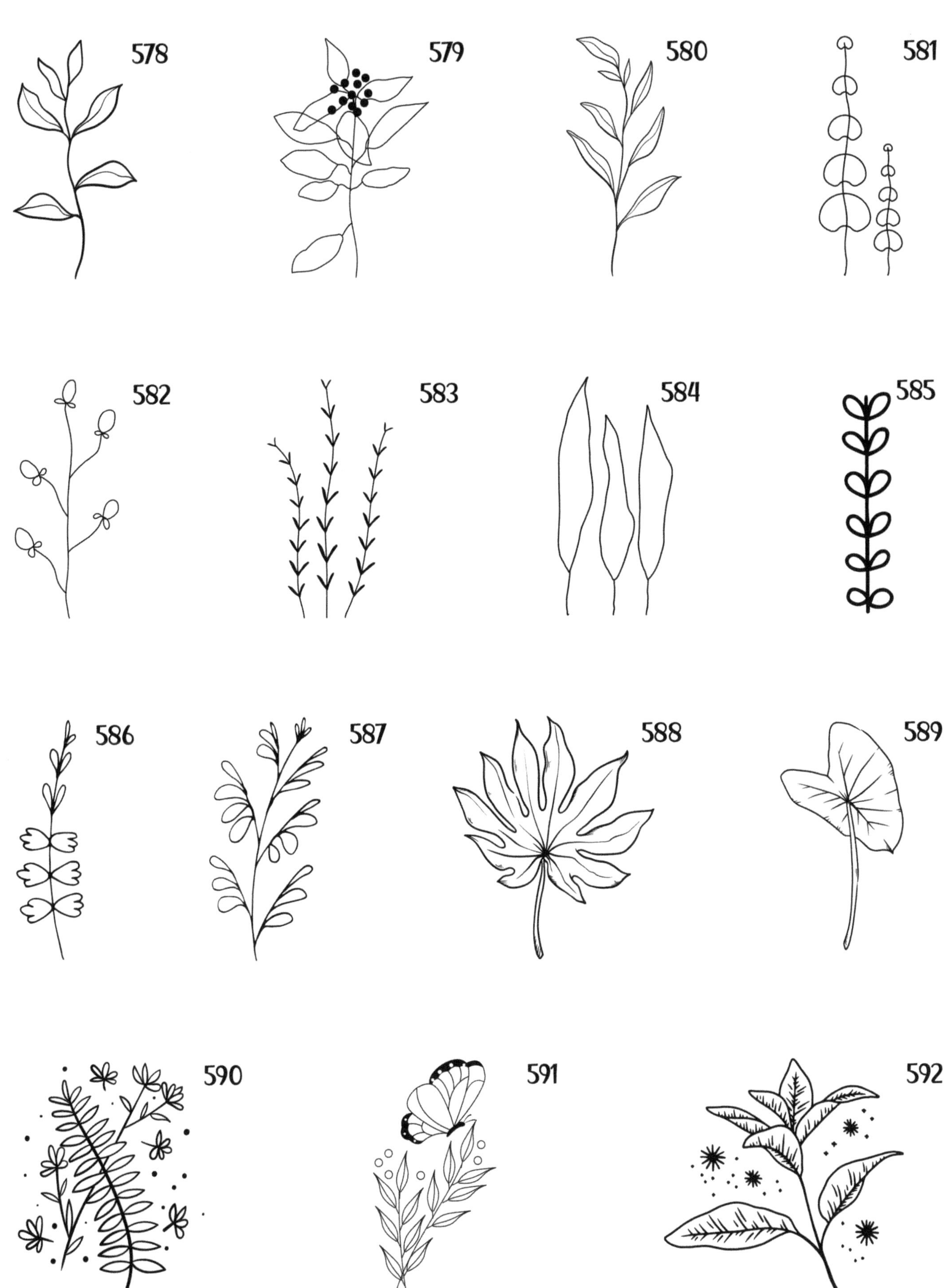

578
579
580
581
582
583
584
585
586
587
588
589
590
591
592

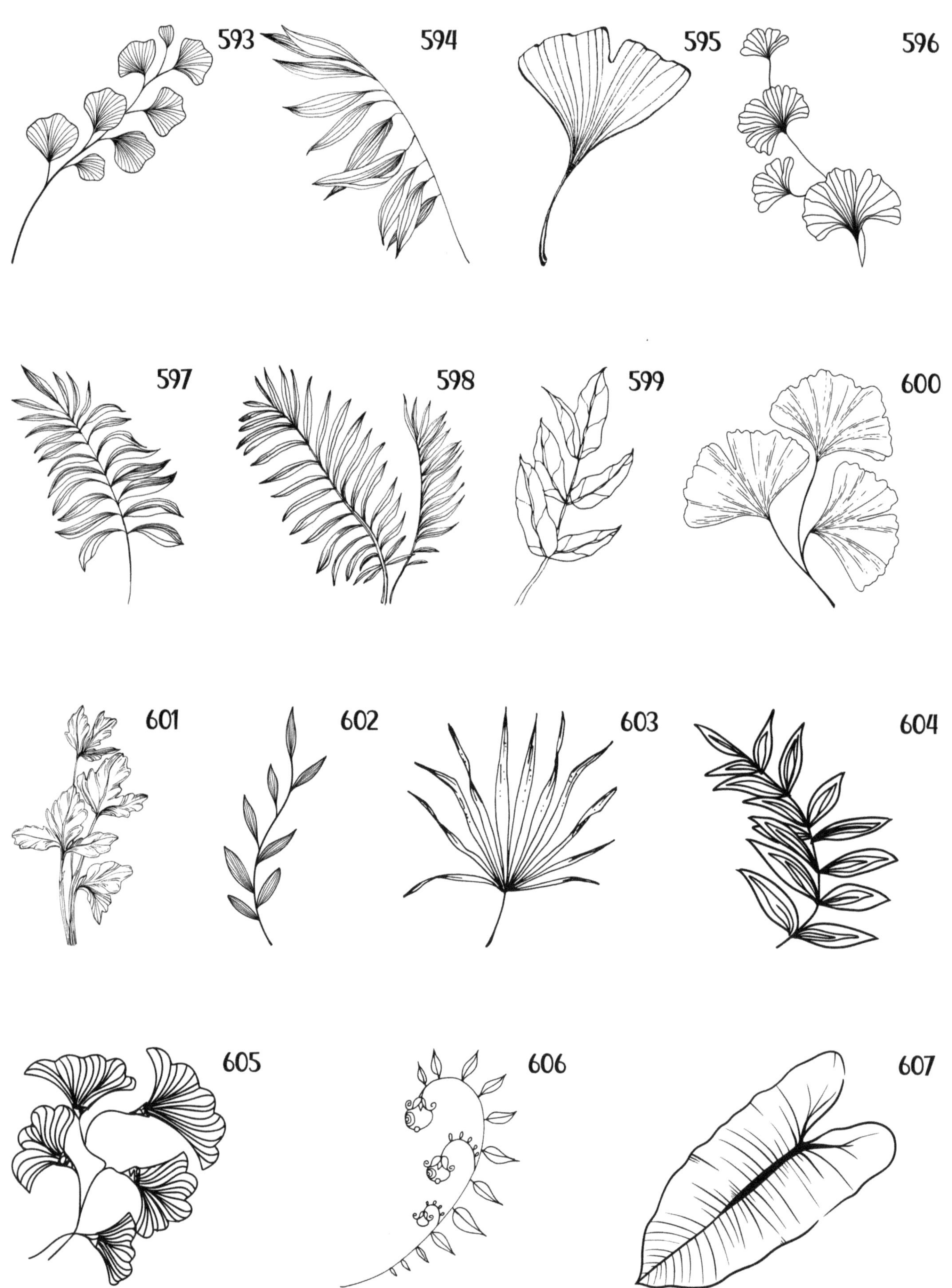

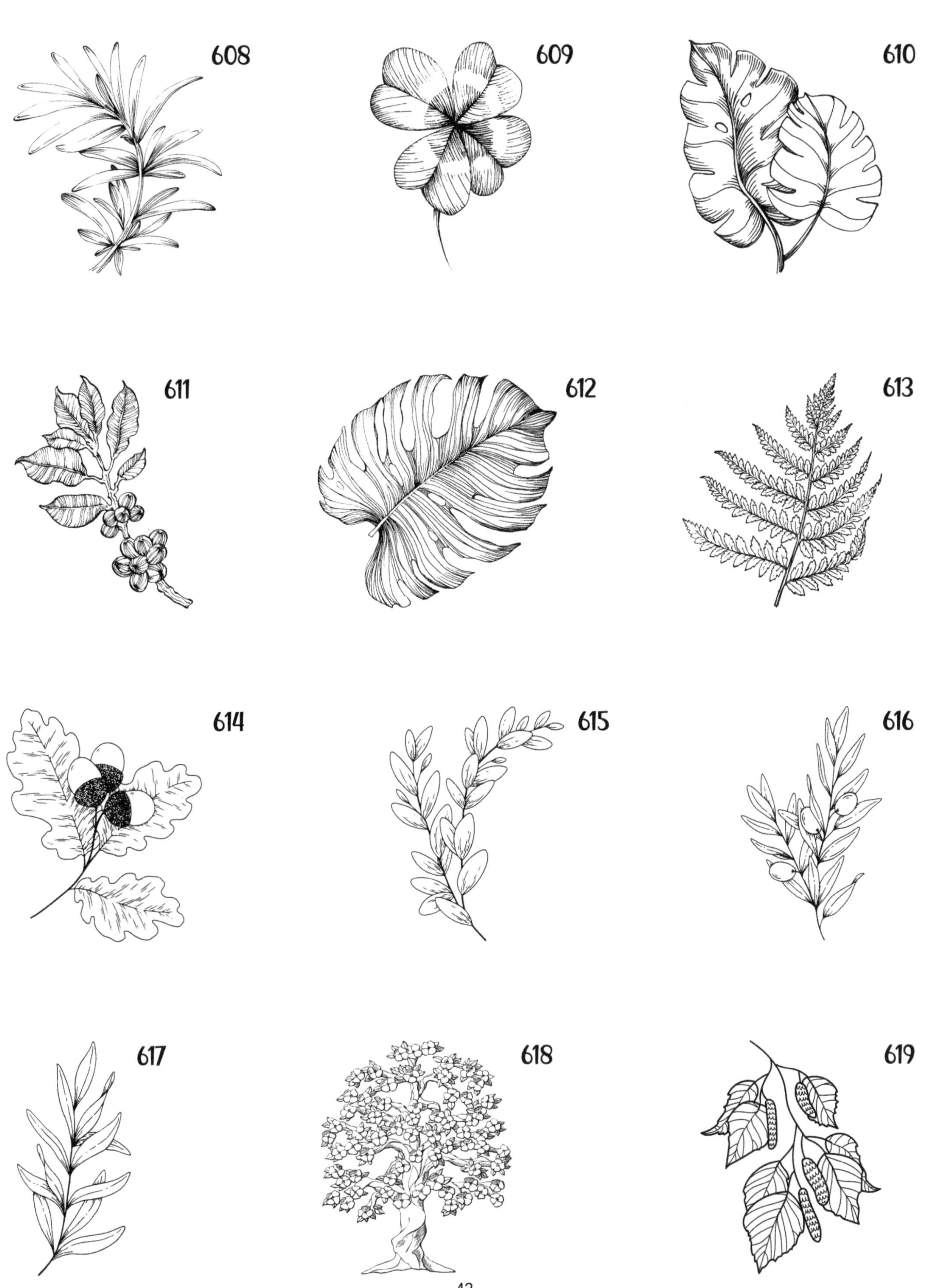
608
609
610
611
612
613
614
615
616
617
618
619

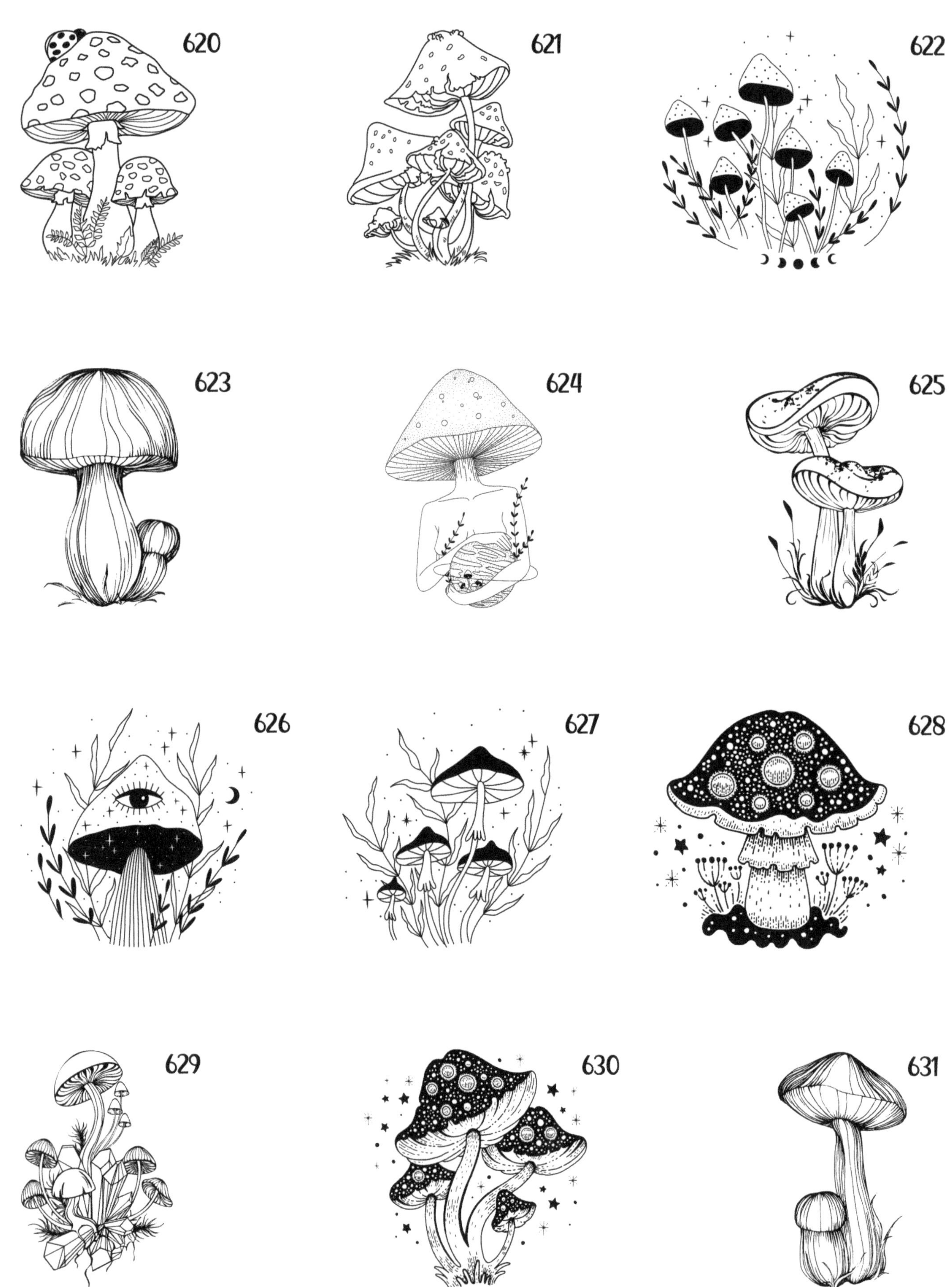

620
621
622
623
624
625
626
627
628
629
630
631

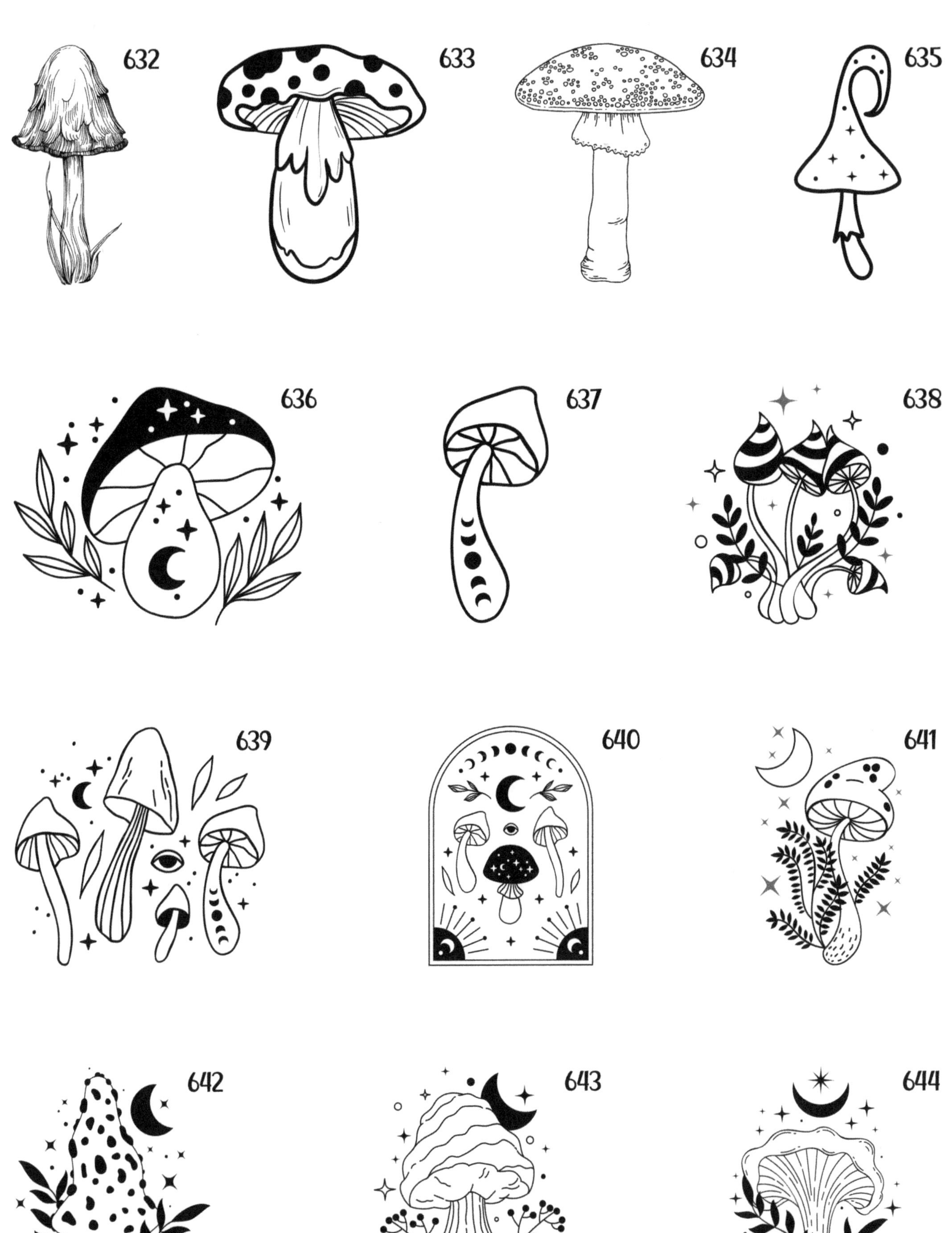

632
633
634
635
636
637
638
639
640
641
642
643
644

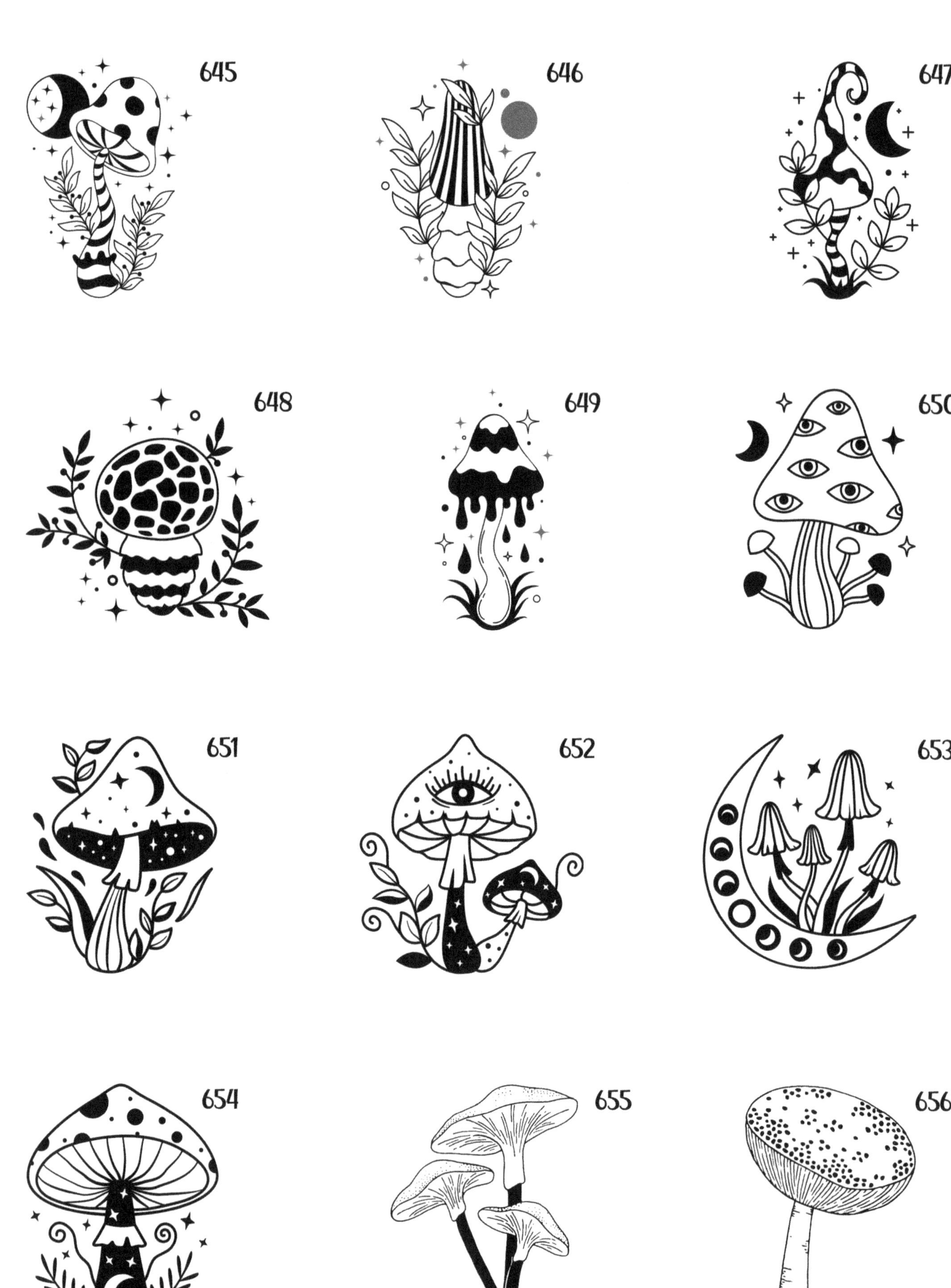

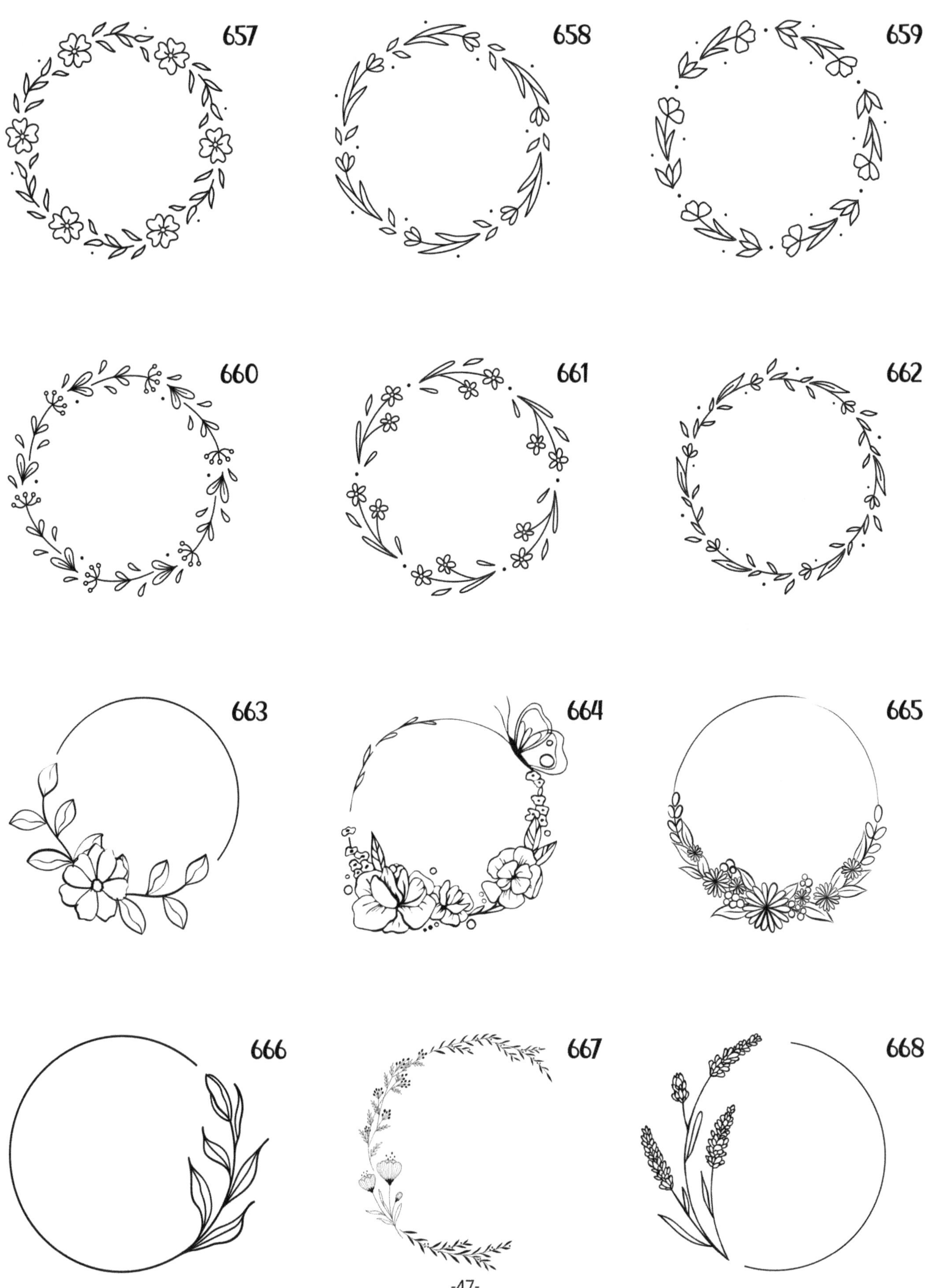

657

658

659

660

661

662

663

664

665

666

667

668

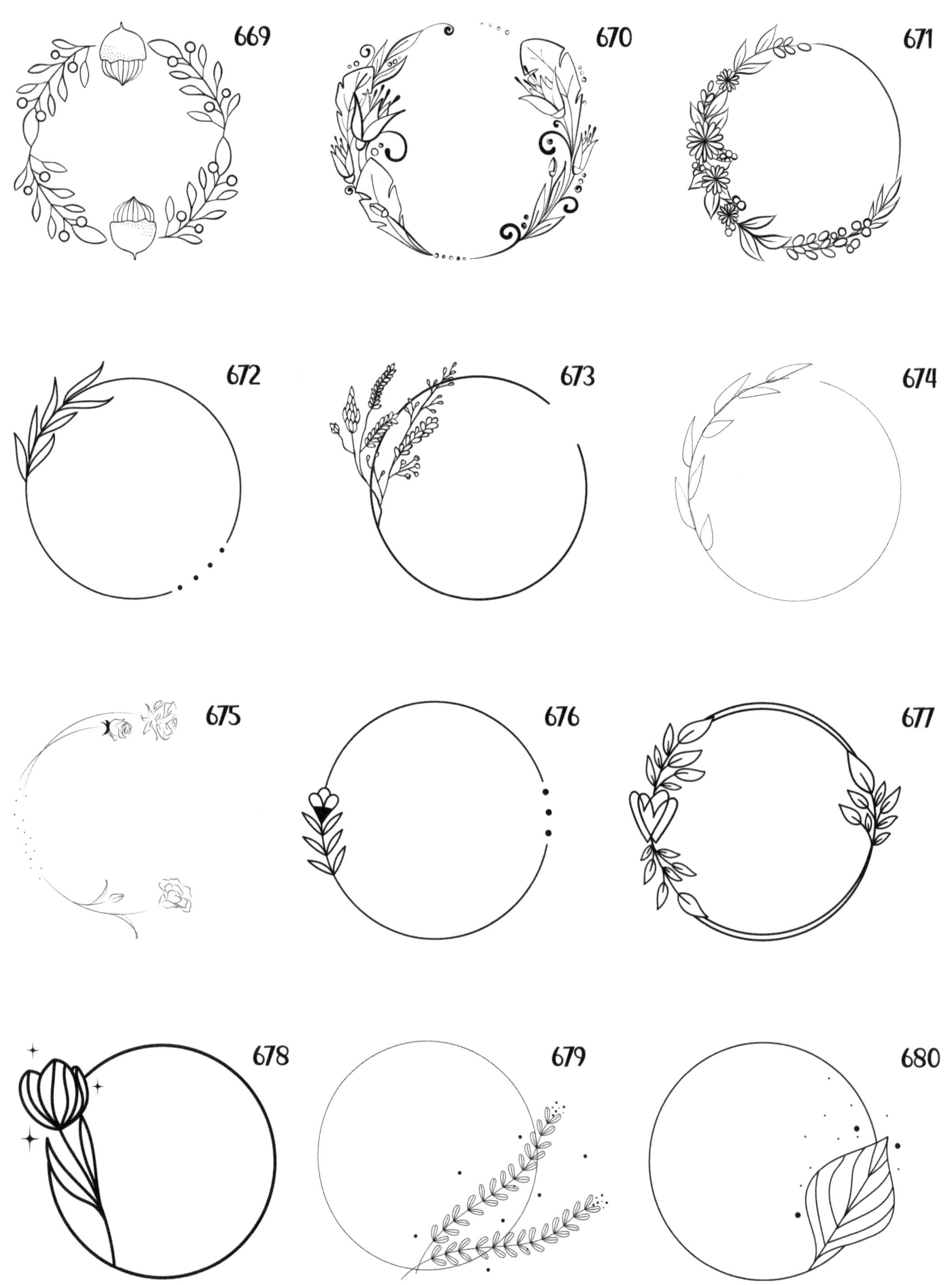
669
670
671
672
673
674
675
676
677
678
679
680

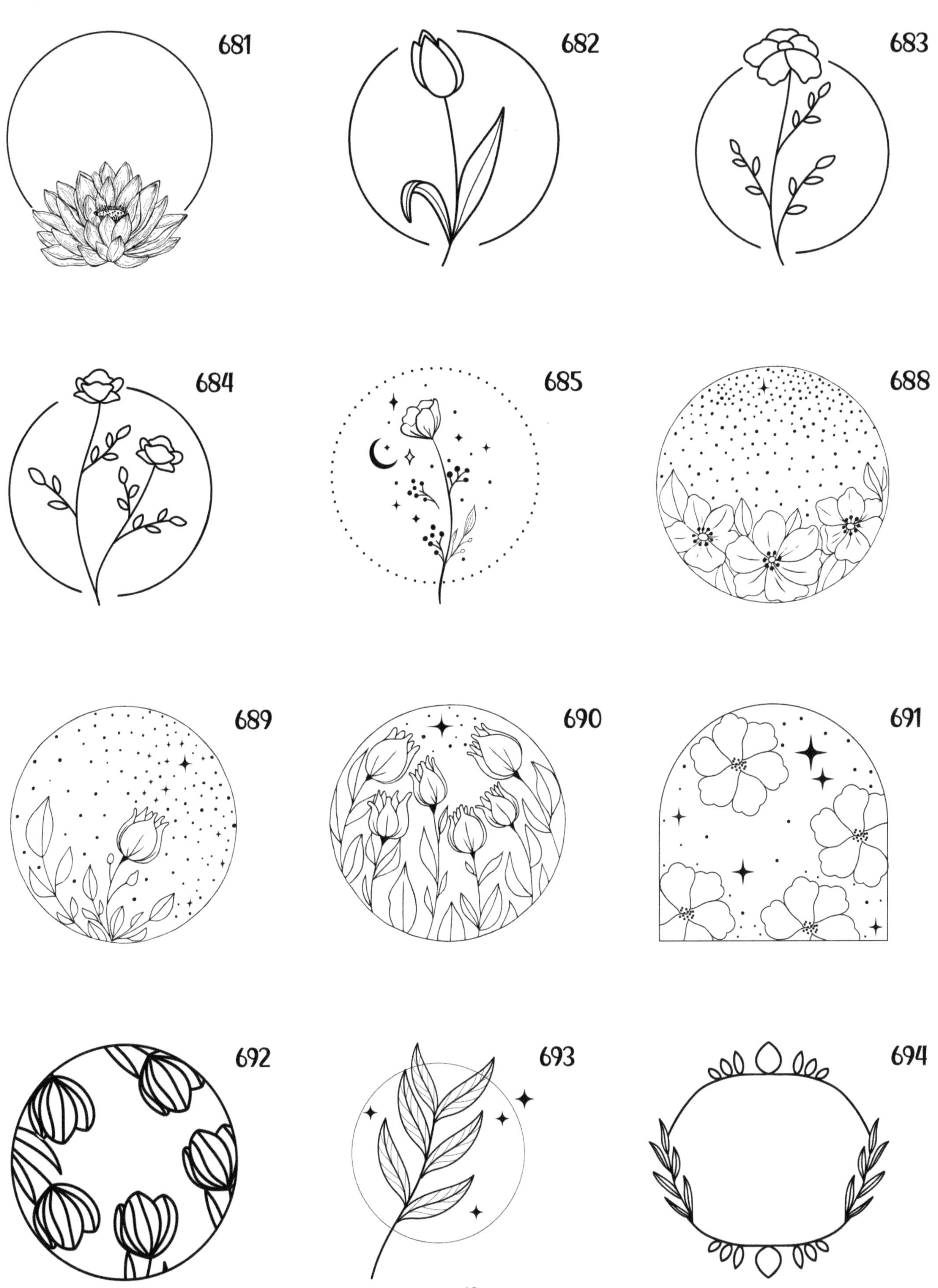

681
682
683
684
685
688
689
690
691
692
693
694

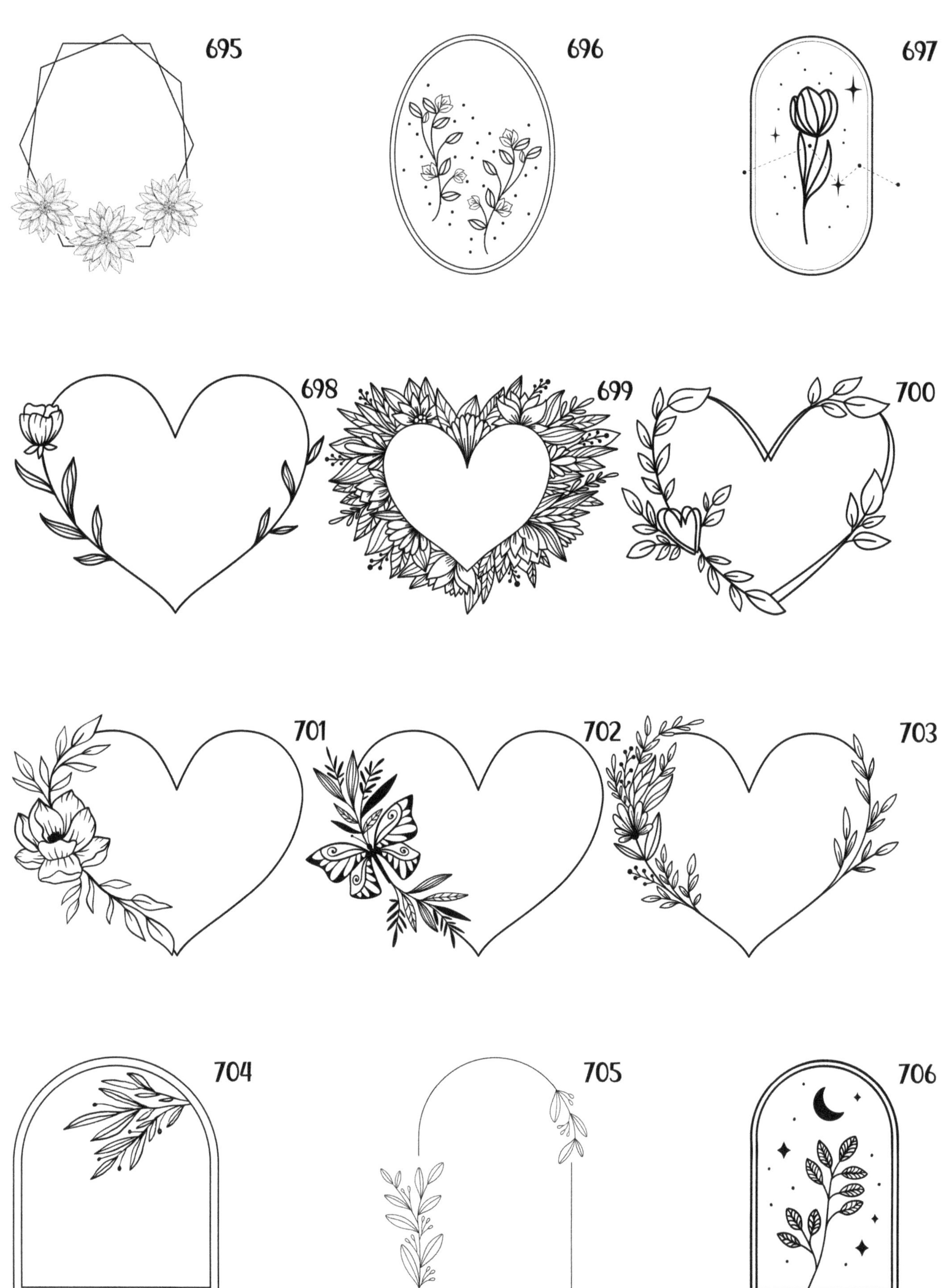
695
696
697
698
699
700
701
702
703
704
705
706

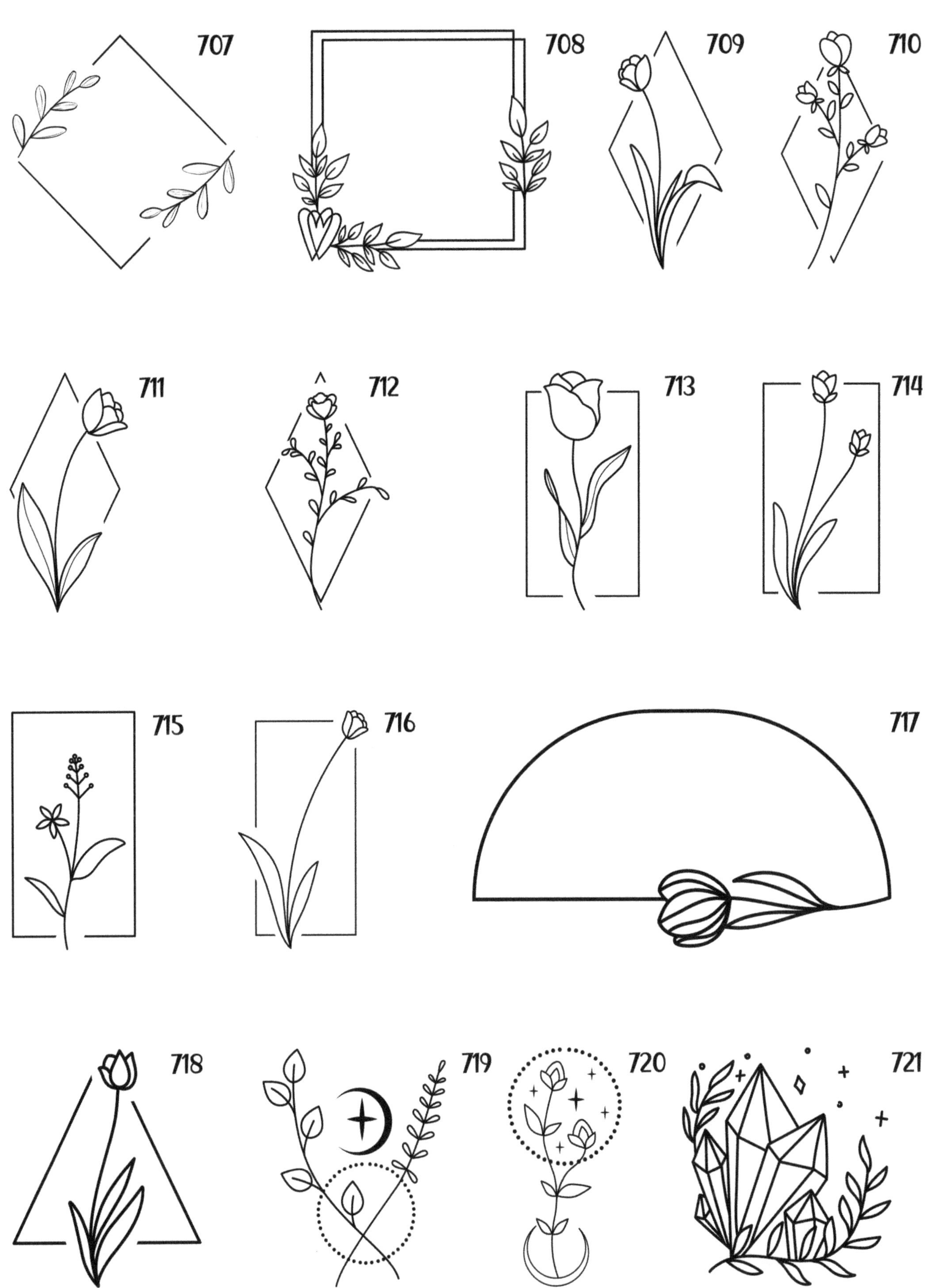
707
708
709
710
711
712
713
714
715
716
717
718
719
720
721

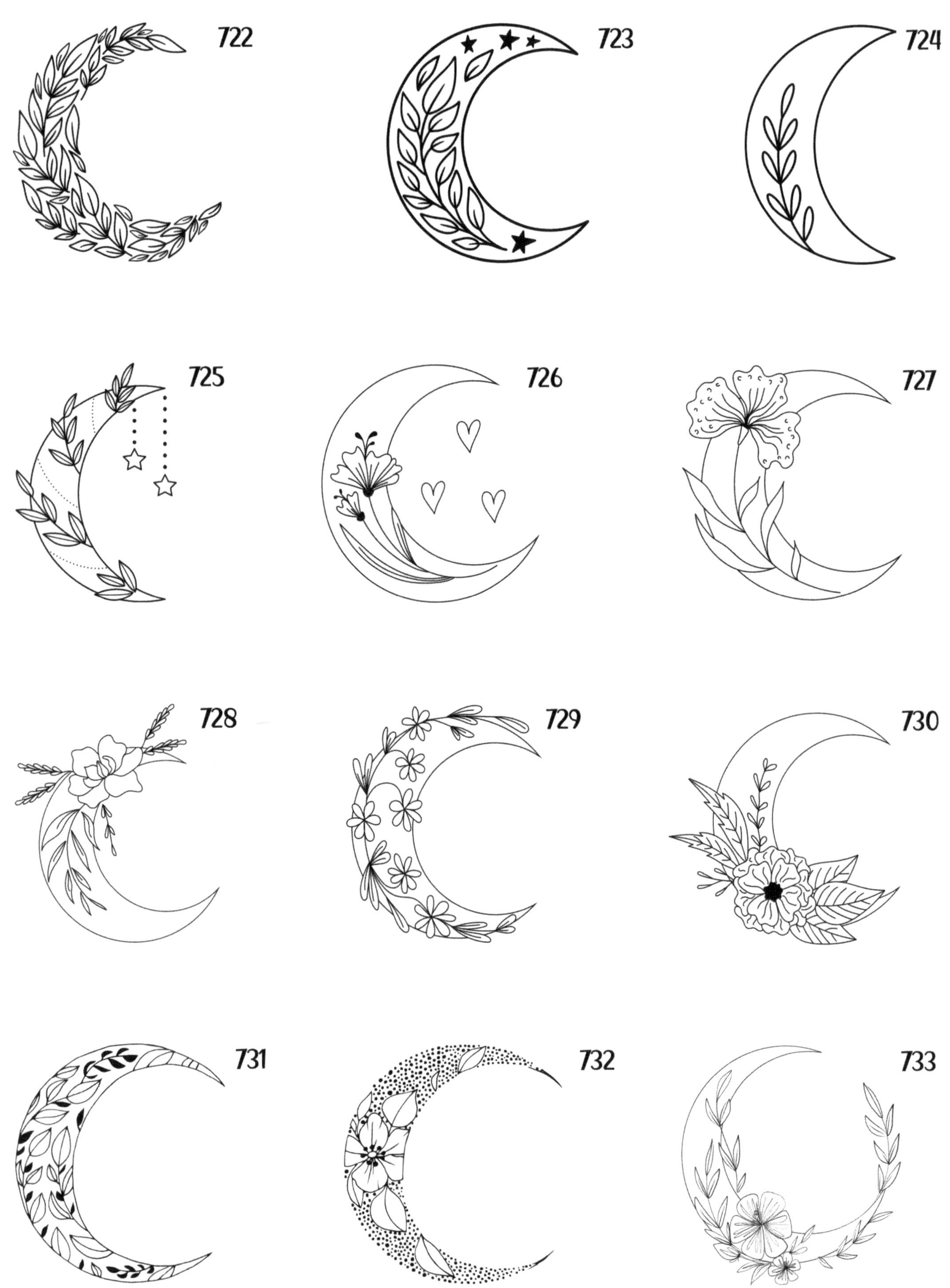

722
723
724
725
726
727
728
729
730
731
732
733

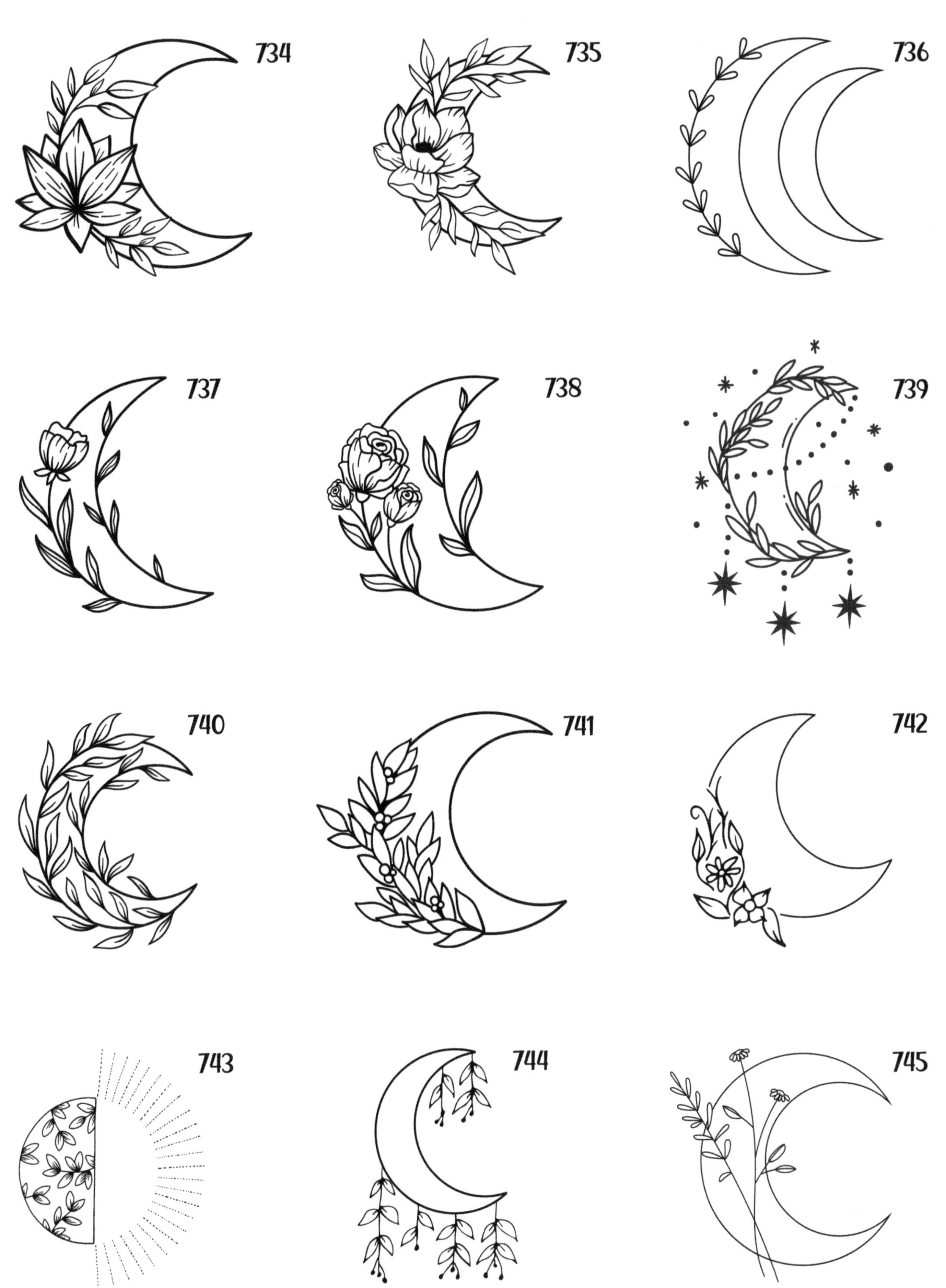

734
735
736
737
738
739
740
741
742
743
744
745

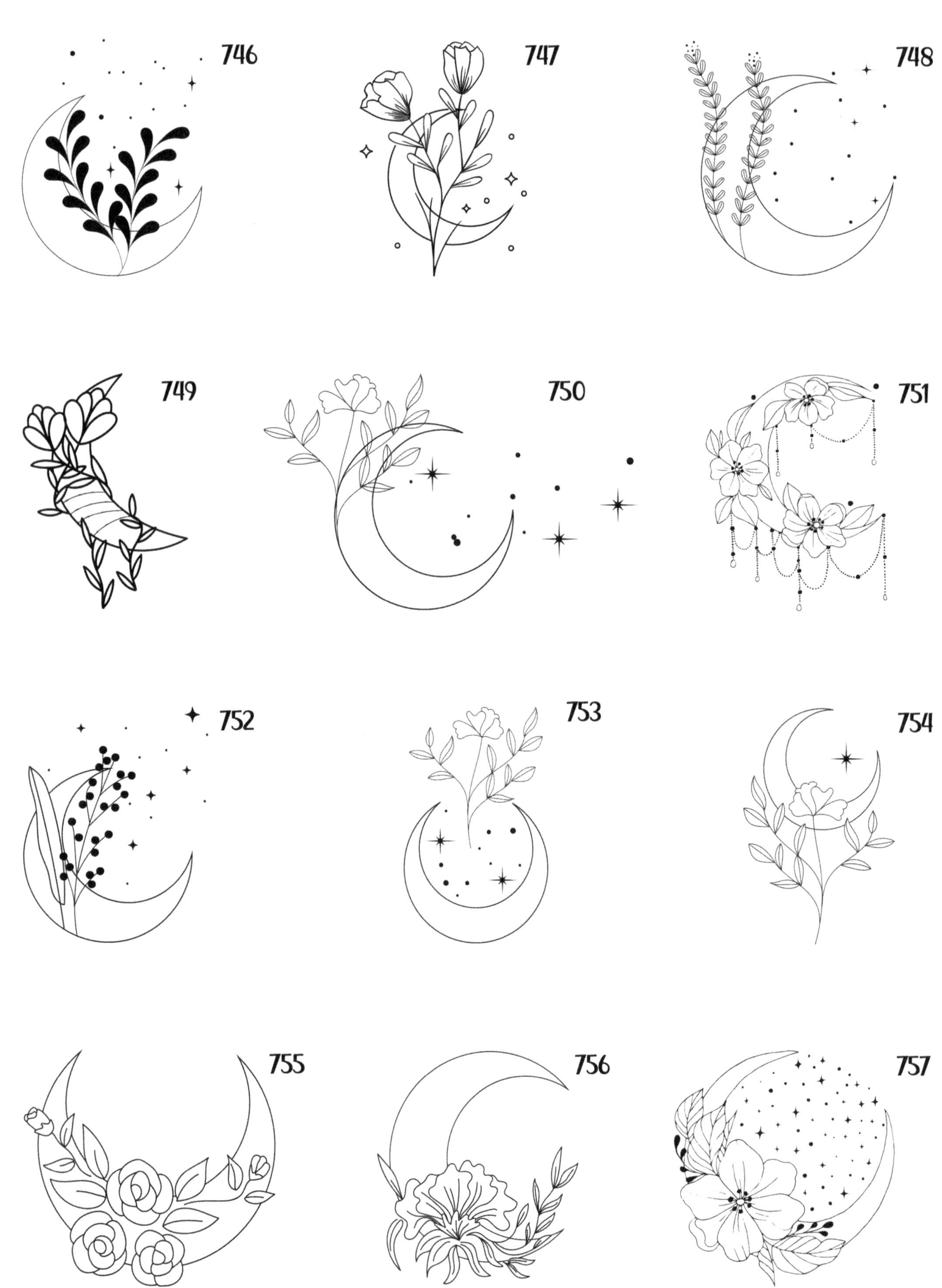

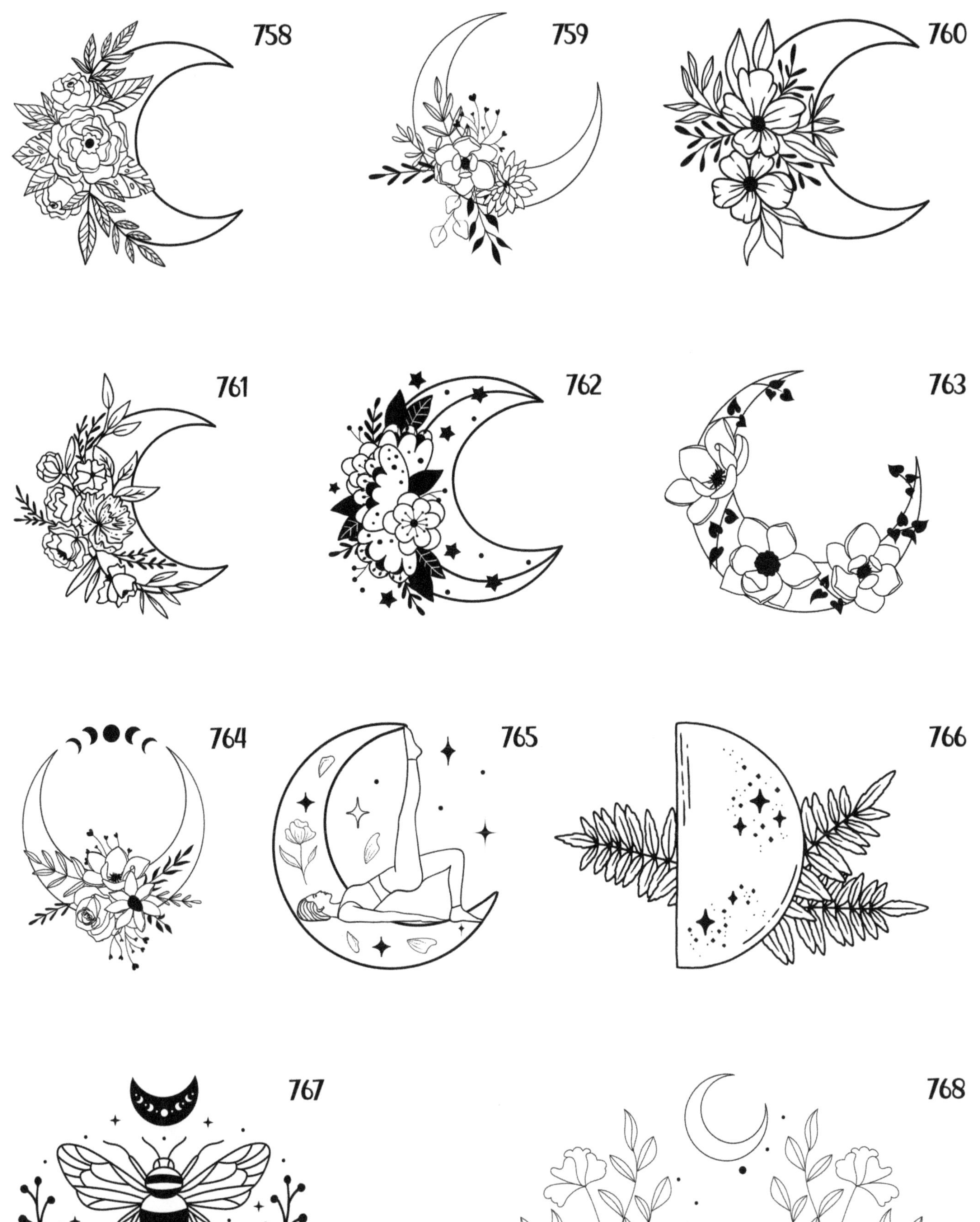

758
759
760
761
762
763
764
765
766
767
768

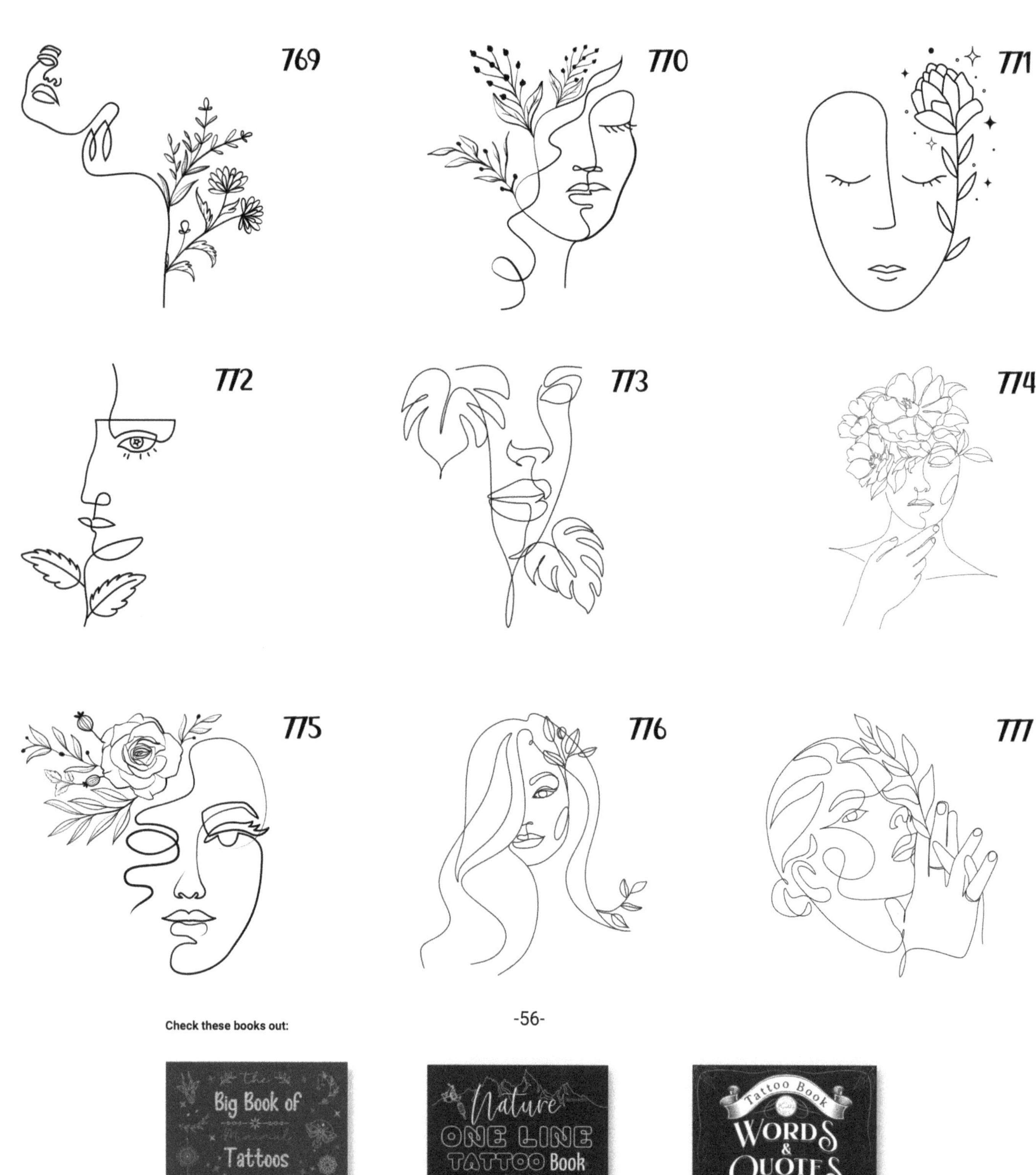

Check these books out:

Impressum

Kohls Digiworx
vertreten durch:
Martina Kohls, Lindenstrasse 5, 57648 Bölsberg
Deutschland
ISBN: 978-3-910363-03-8
Independently Published
This book was printed by IngramSpark©